Getting My Ducks In A Row

Building Bridges
Setting Guideposts
Leaving a Legacy

Douglas G. Goldberg

Copyright @ 2004 by Black Rhino Publications, LLC. No part of this book may be reproduced or used in any form or by any means, electronic or mechanical, including photocopying, recording, or by any information or retrieval system, without the prior written permission of the author. Printed in the United States of America.

ISBN 0976439816 (ISBN-10) and 978-0-9764398-1-3 (ISBN-13)

Published by Black Rhino Publications, LLC

629 N. Weber Street, Suite 1
Colorado Springs, CO 80903-1077

719-444-0300

www.goldberglawcenter.com

Table of Contents

Preface 1

My Family and Me 4

    Personal Information 5
    Child-Care Information 8
    Pet Profile 10
    Document Locator 14
    Household Items Location 18
    Relatives and Friends 19
    Advisors 21
    Fiduciary Review 25
    Estate Plan Review Checklist 28

My Finances and Insurance 31

    Funding Review 33
    Real Estate Information 34
    Investment Account Information 38
    Retirement Plan Information 42
    Education Savings Accounts 44
    Annuity Contracts 48
    Bank Account Information 52
    Automobile Information 56
    Business Information 60
    Personal Property 66
    Safe Deposit Box 70
    Internet Account Access 72
    Credit Card Information 76
    Other Loan Information 79

Life Insurance	81
Health and Major Medical Insurance	85
Disability Insurance Information	87
Property Insurance	91
Automobile Insurance	93
Other Insurances	96

If I'm Disabled — 99

Disability Guidelines	101
Disability Instructions & Guidelines	102
Letter of Instruction to My Health Care Representative	104
Medical Intervention Definitions	115
Hypothetical Scenario Analysis	116
Do Not Resuscitate Notice	120
Disability Checklist For Me	121
Disability Checklist For Helpers	122

After I'm Gone — 125

First Steps When Someone Dies	127
Memorandum for Distribution of Tangible Personal Property	131
Letter of Instruction to My Guardian and Trustee	133
Social Security	143
Instructions for Final Arrangements	144
To My Loved Ones	145

Preface

The phrase "getting your ducks in a row" is about getting things organized, prepared and properly arranged. That's what this book is all about. It's about organizing your personal and financial affairs and leaving detailed instructions for your family so that if and when you become disabled or die, your family can spend their time remembering what a wonderful person you were and celebrating your life, rather than embarking on a long, frustrating and potentially expensive treasure hunt to determine what you own, how much it is worth, where the records are kept, and to whom they should speak for advice.

Anything worthwhile is not easily or quickly accomplished. Some people don't even know they have any ducks. But you do. You've already taken the first step to getting your ducks in a row. You've opened this book!

It's also likely that you are in the process of, or perhaps have already completed, the hardest part of the whole process – designing and implementing your estate plan. Finishing that process will catapult you into the top 30% of Americans who care about their families. That's right! In the age of the internet, documents on disc and information at your fingertips, approximately 70% of Americans do absolutely no estate planning. They spend more time planning their next vacation than planning for their family's future without them and give up the control of their family's future to the government.

And even if they have completed some planning, chances are good that it's not current. If the planning was done over three years ago, it will likely be outdated. Like the car that was purchased brand new but hasn't had the oil changed for over 50,000 miles, the plan may work, but not as originally intended and certainly not as well as it could.

That's where this book comes in. It is a living, loving and constantly evolving book that you write for your family. Properly completed and regularly updated, it will keep all your important information in one easily accessible place. It can be a great tool for consolidation of your personal and financial information and can be of tremendous value to the people who care about you the most.

As with any document you'd prepare on your own, you decide how detailed you want to be. I recommend filling out all the sections and updating every year. Maybe you can update it when you review your financial matters, your insurance and your will. Maybe toward the end of the year while working on your goals for the New Year, or around tax time.

Getting My Ducks in a Row is one of the most comprehensive, easy to use tools available to help you organize your affairs and prepare for the unexpected. I have been an estate planning attorney for over 25 years and have helped hundreds of families sort through the mess when a loved one becomes mentally disabled or dies unprepared.

The book includes worksheets to record details relating to your financial, legal and insurance affairs. It offers you an opportunity to give step-by-step guidance for your heirs if you become mentally incapacitated, instructions for your medical care, worksheets to record funeral preferences and obituary information, a comprehensive document locator system, and much more. Once completed, you'll feel a great sense of accomplishment and peace of mind knowing you're not going to leave your grieving family in a state of chaos. Sometimes planning for the unexpected involves asking the question "What if I died unexpectedly?" Just as important, however, is: "What if I live for a really, really, really long time?" This book can help on both fronts.

Getting My Ducks in a Row will help you and your family accomplish three very important things:

1. Save money. Attorneys, accountants and financial advisors charge thousands to organize estates. A good portion of these expenses involve time spent tracking down records of what people own, what they owe, who is in charge, how do things get paid for, and who should receive the property when they die. Completing the forms in this book will save your family a great deal of money because everything will already be organized.

2. Save those you love a lot of grief. Loss of a loved one is tough enough on a grieving family. Sadly, the pain, stress, aggravation, family quarrels, lost time and wasted money that result from poor planning can multiply that sorrow. Completing this book will help to clarify communication and will lay out a roadmap for your family to follow. Putting everything in order before a tragedy will not only

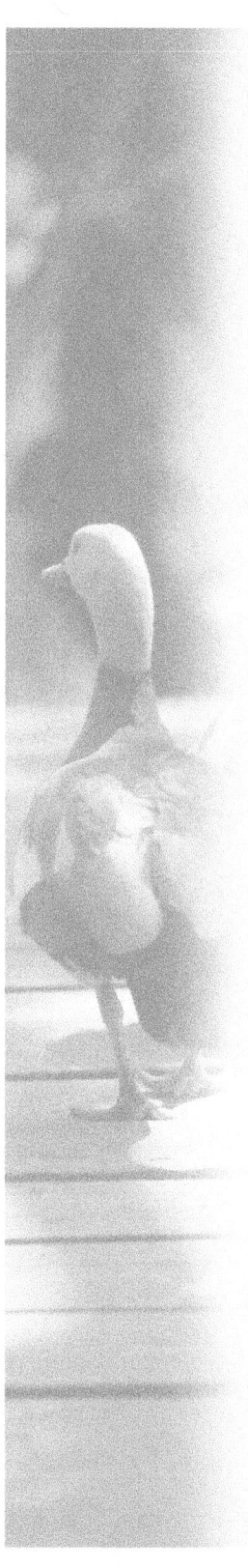

simplify things for your family, it will clearly express how much you love them.

3. Avoid legal and financial pitfalls. No one is an expert at everything. The wisest people are those who avoid mistakes by knowing when to seek advice. I have helped hundreds of families put the many pieces of their financial and legal planning in order. That knowledge and experience is built into this book and it is intended to help your family succeed in planning and make smart decisions.

Do this project with your family or by yourself. Do it at your kitchen table or at your favorite restaurant or coffee house. But as the Nike ad says, JUST DO IT. It may well be one of the most thoughtful and loving things you ever do for your family.

Douglas G. Goldberg

My Family and Me

Personal Information

Name _____

    Maiden _____

Name of Spouse _____

Address _____
Previous Addresses _____

Date of Birth _____ Birth Place _____

Blood Type _____
Medical Allergies _____

Father's Name _____

Mother's Name _____
    Maiden _____

Children   Date of Birth

_____   _____

_____   _____

_____   _____

_____   _____

Brothers and Sisters   Spouse

_____   _____
_____   _____
_____   _____
_____   _____
_____   _____

Date   Major Illness/Surgery   Attending Physician

_____   _____   _____
_____   _____   _____
_____   _____   _____
_____   _____   _____
_____   _____   _____

Branch of Military Service _____

Enlistment Date _____

Discharge Date/Rank _____

Occupation _____

_____

Employed By _____

Schools Attended

_____
High School   City   State   Degree/Date

_____
College   City   State   Degree/Date

_____
Other   City   State   Degree/Date

6   *Getting My Ducks In A Row*

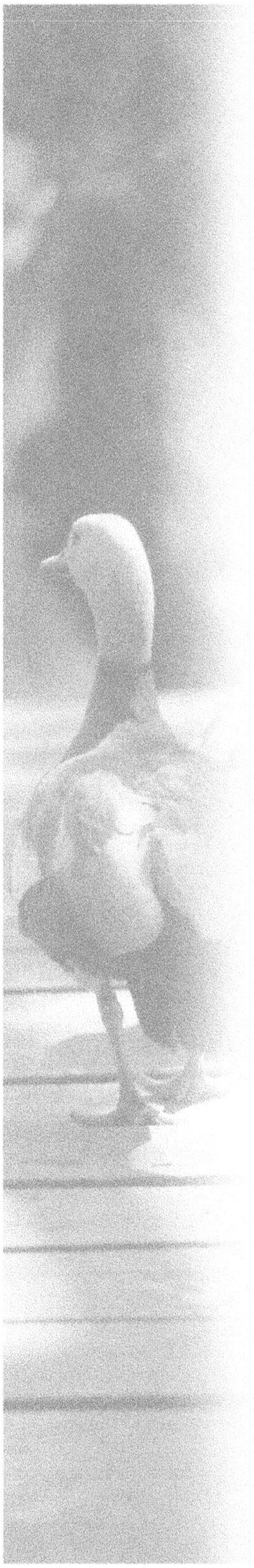

Church Membership _____

Affiliation _____

Fraternal, Service, Social, and Union Memberships _____
_____
_____
_____

Special Recognition/Other Information _____
_____
_____
_____
_____
_____
_____

Notes _____
_____
_____
_____
_____
_____
_____
_____
_____
_____
_____
_____

My Family and Me

Child-Care Information

Children

Name   Age   Medications/Diet/Other Information

_____

_____

_____

_____

_____

Schools and/or Day Care Providers

Name _____ Principal _____

Address _____

City _____ State _____ Zip _____

Phone (_____) _____

Name _____ Principal _____

Address _____

City _____ State _____ Zip _____

Phone (_____) _____

Contact Information in Case of Emergency

Name _____

Cell phone number for emergency caregiver (_____) _____

Name _____

Cell phone for alternate emergency caregiver (_____) _____

If you are unable to reach the emergency contacts, please contact:

_____ Home Phone Number (_____)_____

_____ Work Phone Number (_____)_____

Other information

Food/snack preferences, grooming, exercise, play, and safety precautions, fears, habits, medical conditions, medical requirements, special care needs, favorite toys, etc.:

_____
_____
_____
_____
_____
_____
_____
_____
_____
_____
_____
_____
_____
_____
_____
_____
_____
_____
_____
_____

Pet Profile

Identification

My Pet's Name

_____

Type of Animal

_____

Sex   ❑ M   ❑ F

Spayed / Neutered

Month / Year of Birth

_____ / _____

Place
Photograph
Here

Normal Weight _____

Brief description, including breed information:

_____

_____

My pet has the following identification:

❑ Microchip ID – Number _____

❑ License – Number _____

❑ Tattoo – Number or mark _____

❑ Other _____

My pet's veterinarian _____

Clinic _____ Phone (____) _____

Behavior

My pet has the following preferences, dislikes, fears or habits:

_____

_____

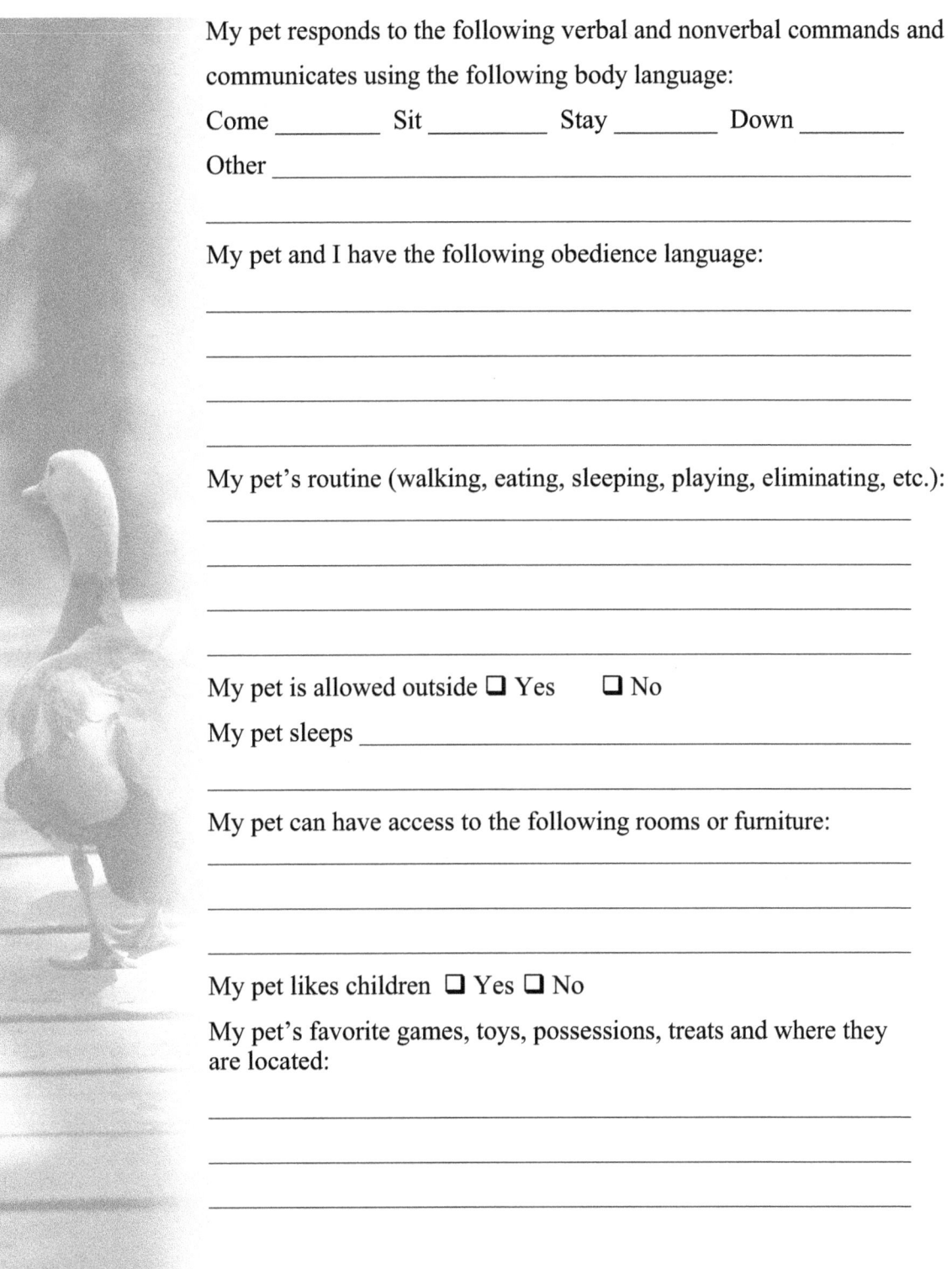

My pet responds to the following verbal and nonverbal commands and communicates using the following body language:

Come _____ Sit _____ Stay _____ Down _____
Other _____
_____

My pet and I have the following obedience language:

_____
_____
_____

My pet's routine (walking, eating, sleeping, playing, eliminating, etc.):

_____
_____
_____

My pet is allowed outside ❑ Yes   ❑ No

My pet sleeps _____
_____

My pet can have access to the following rooms or furniture:

_____
_____
_____

My pet likes children ❑ Yes ❑ No

My pet's favorite games, toys, possessions, treats and where they are located:

_____
_____
_____

Pet Profile

Health

Following is my pet's health history:
_____
_____
_____

My pet has the following recurring health problems:
_____
_____
_____

My pet currently takes the following medications:
_____
_____
_____

My pet takes the following type of flea / heartworm preventative:
_____

My pet has the following special diet needs:
_____
_____
_____

My pet has the following allergies to foods, medications, fleas, flea control products, etc.:
_____
_____

Special care instructions

Document Locator

Estate Planning Portfolio Location

_____

Home Address:_____

Safety Deposit Box:_____
Box Number:_____
Bank:_____

_____

Key Location:_____

Attorney   _____

                    _____

Accountant   _____

                    _____

Financial Advisor_____

                    _____

Insurance Advisor_____

                    _____

Real Estate Agent_____

                    _____

Estate Planning Document Locations

Living Trust   _____
Original Will   _____
Copies of Will   _____

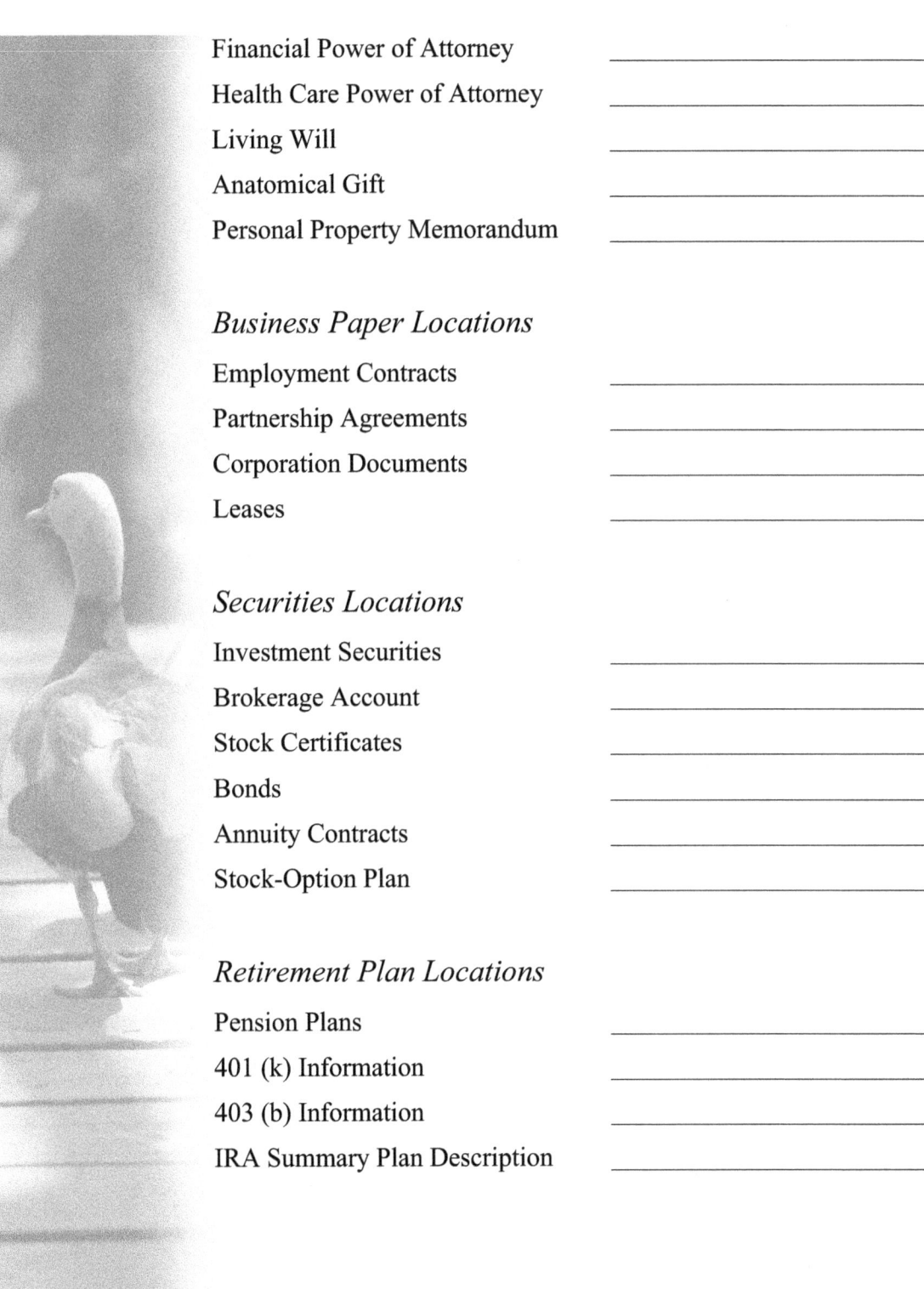

Financial Power of Attorney _____
Health Care Power of Attorney _____
Living Will _____
Anatomical Gift _____
Personal Property Memorandum _____

Business Paper Locations

Employment Contracts _____
Partnership Agreements _____
Corporation Documents _____
Leases _____

Securities Locations

Investment Securities _____
Brokerage Account _____
Stock Certificates _____
Bonds _____
Annuity Contracts _____
Stock-Option Plan _____

Retirement Plan Locations

Pension Plans _____
401 (k) Information _____
403 (b) Information _____
IRA Summary Plan Description _____

Cash Locations

Checkbook(s)   _____

Savings Passbook(s)   _____

Credit Cards   _____

CDs   _____

Bank Statements   _____

Tax Record Locations

Income Tax Returns   _____

Gift Tax Returns   _____

Real Estate Information Locations

Deeds to Real Estate   _____

Mortgages   _____

Cemetery Plot Deed   _____

Notes & Loan Agreements   _____

Rental Property Agreements   _____

  _____

Personal Effects and Other Asset Locations

Distribution Memorandum   _____

Car Titles   _____

Boat/Plane Titles   _____

Social Security Card   _____

Financial Records/Passwords   _____

List of Insurance Policies   _____

Marriage Certificate   _____

Divorce/Separation Papers   _____
Birth Certificates   _____
Adoption Papers   _____
Citizenship Papers   _____
Military Papers   _____
Contact Lists   _____
Other   _____
Other   _____
Other   _____
Other   _____
Other   _____
Other   _____

Notes: _____

_____
_____
_____
_____
_____
_____
_____
_____
_____
_____
_____
_____
_____

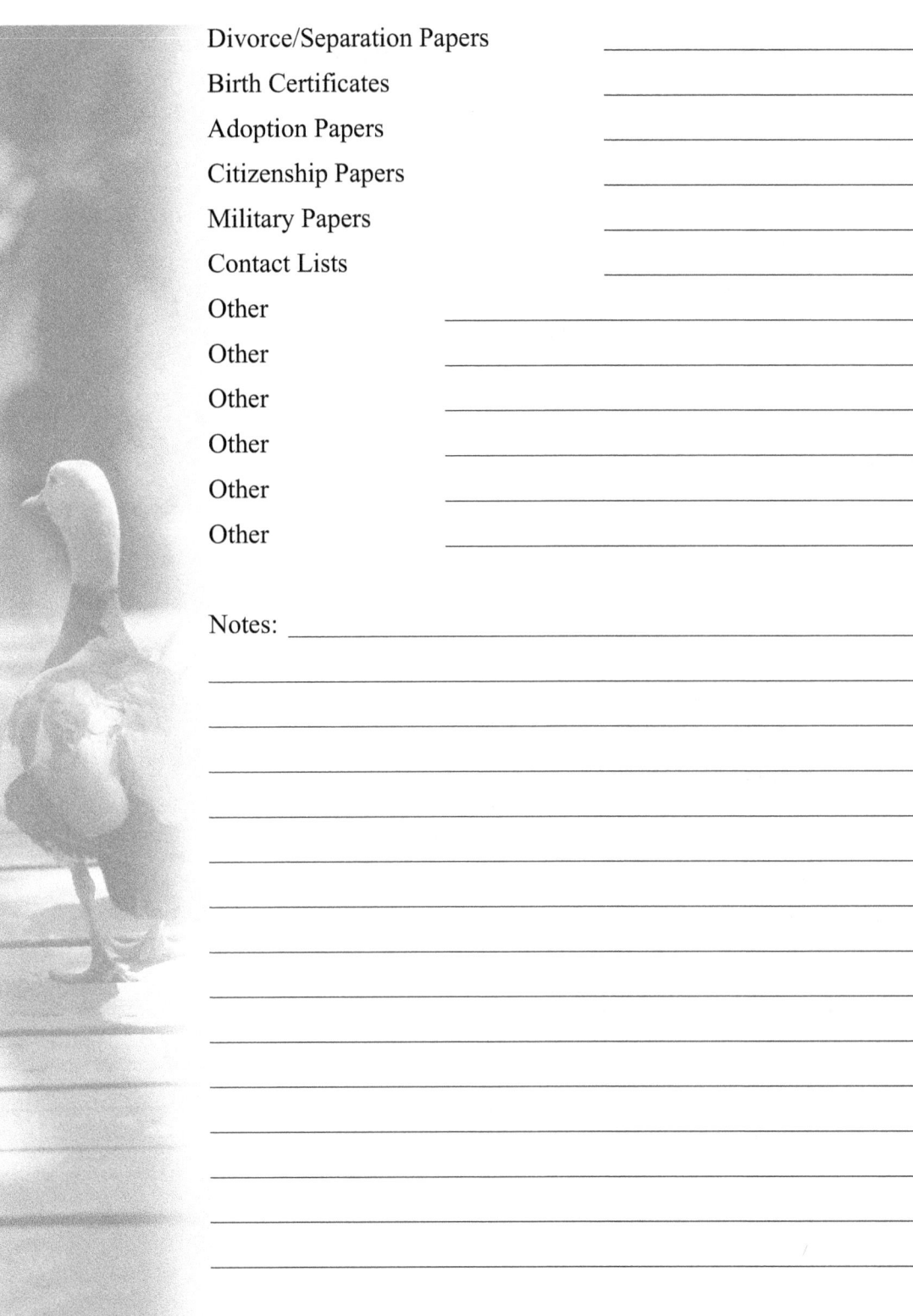

My Family and Me

Household Items Location

Car Keys _____

House Keys _____

Storage Unit Keys _____

Safety Deposit Box Keys _____

Alarm System Box Instructions/Details_____

_____

_____

Electrical Breaker Box _____

Thermostat _____

Water Shut-off _____

Sprinkler System Panel/Box _____

My computer passwords are located: _____

_____

_____

My computer email addresses and passwords are located:

_____

_____

My telephone password(s) _____

_____

Other important stuff you need to know:

_____

_____

_____

_____

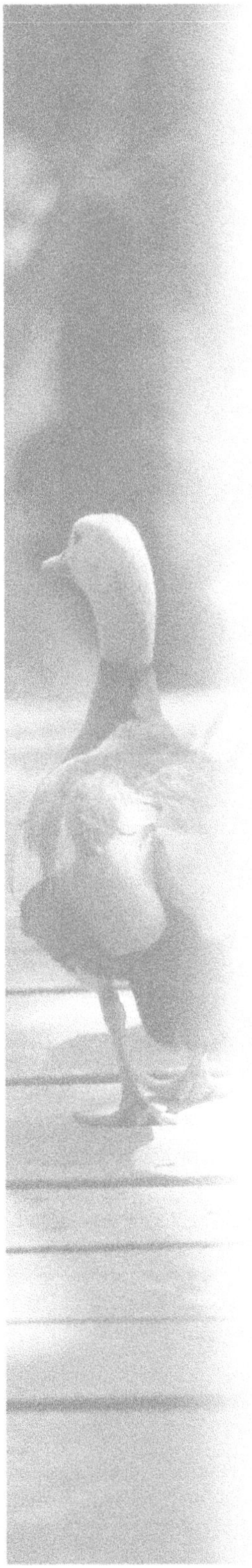

Relatives and Friends

Name _____

Home Phone (_____)_____ Work (_____)_____

Address_____

Name _____

Home Phone (_____)_____ Work (_____)_____

Address_____

Name _____

Home Phone (_____)_____ Work (_____)_____

Address_____

Name _____

Home Phone (_____)_____ Work (_____)_____

Address_____

Name _____

Home Phone (_____)_____ Work (_____)_____

Address_____

Name _____

Home Phone (_____)_____ Work (_____)_____

Address_____

Name _____
Home Phone (_____)_____ Work (_____)_____
Address _____

Name _____
Home Phone (_____)_____ Work (_____)_____
Address _____

Name _____
Home Phone (_____)_____ Work (_____)_____
Address _____

Name _____
Home Phone (_____)_____ Work (_____)_____
Address _____

Name _____
Home Phone (_____)_____ Work (_____)_____
Address _____

Name _____
Home Phone (_____)_____ Work (_____)_____
Address _____

Name _____
Home Phone (_____)_____ Work (_____)_____
Address _____

Advisors

Accountant _____

Work Phone (_____)_____ Cell (_____)_____

Address _____

Attorney _____

Work Phone (_____)_____ Cell (_____)_____

Address _____

Auto Insurance Agent _____

Work Phone (_____)_____ Cell (_____)_____

Address _____

Banker _____

Work Phone (_____)_____ Cell (_____)_____

Address _____

Counselor _____

Work Phone (_____)_____ Cell (_____)_____

Address _____

Pastor / Priest / Rabbi _____

Work Phone (_____)_____ Cell (_____)_____

Address _____

Chiropractor _____

Work Phone (_____)_____ Cell (_____)_____

Address _____

Advisors

Doctor _____
Work Phone (_____)_____ Cell (_____)_____
Address _____

Veterinarian _____
Work Phone (_____)_____ Cell (_____)_____
Address _____

Financial Advisor _____
Work Phone (_____)_____ Cell (_____)_____
Address _____

Funeral Director _____
Work Phone (_____)_____ Cell (_____)_____
Address _____

Property Insurance Agent _____
Work Phone (_____)_____ Cell (_____)_____
Address _____

Landlord _____
Work Phone (_____)_____ Cell (_____)_____
Address _____

Life Insurance Agent _____
Work Phone (_____)_____ Cell (_____)_____
Address _____

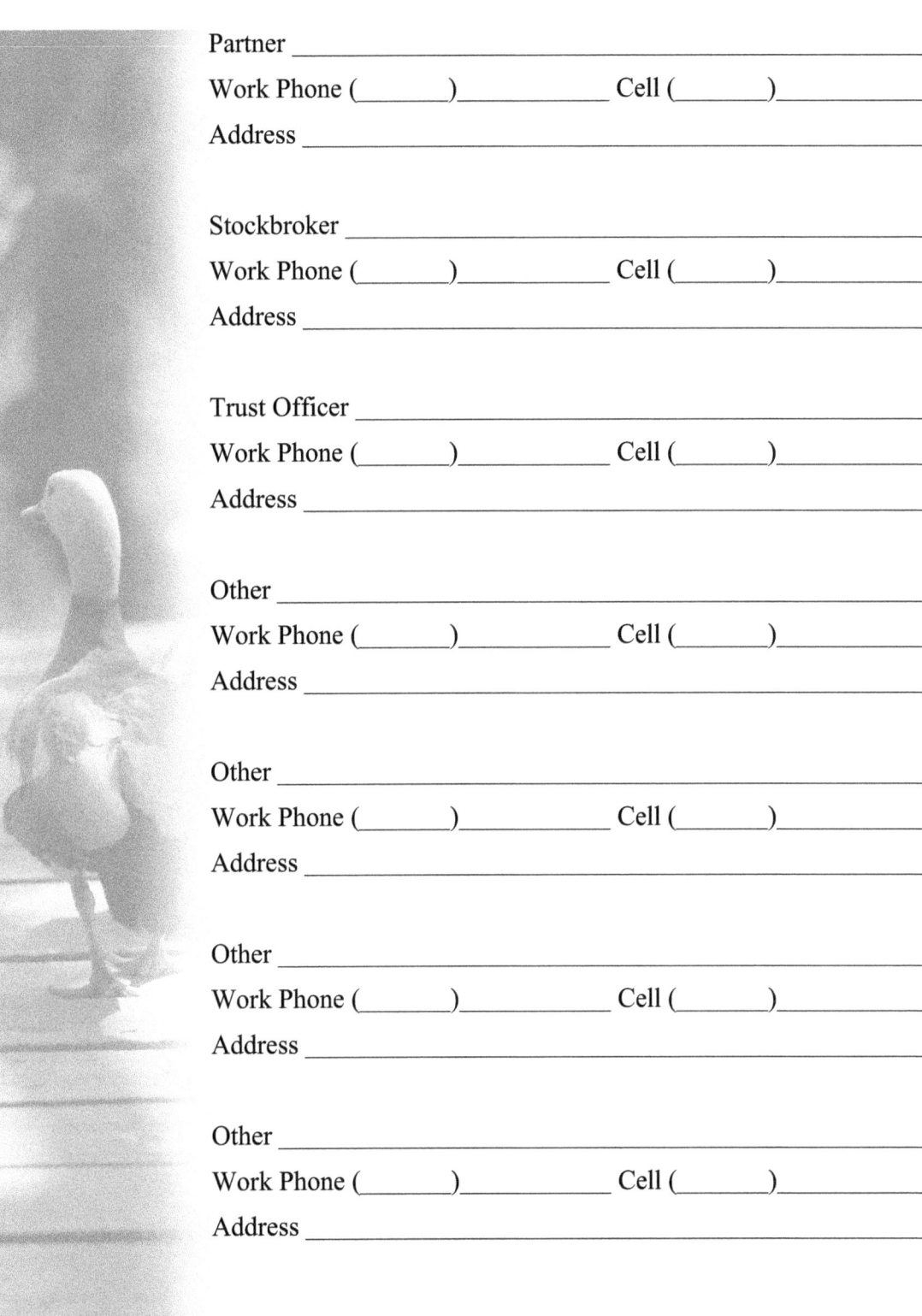

Partner _____
Work Phone (_____)_____ Cell (_____)_____
Address _____

Stockbroker _____
Work Phone (_____)_____ Cell (_____)_____
Address _____

Trust Officer _____
Work Phone (_____)_____ Cell (_____)_____
Address _____

Other _____
Work Phone (_____)_____ Cell (_____)_____
Address _____

Other _____
Work Phone (_____)_____ Cell (_____)_____
Address _____

Other _____
Work Phone (_____)_____ Cell (_____)_____
Address _____

Other _____
Work Phone (_____)_____ Cell (_____)_____
Address _____

Other _____
Work Phone (_____)_____ Cell (_____)_____
Address _____

Other _____
Work Phone (_____)_____ Cell (_____)_____
Address _____

Other _____
Work Phone (_____)_____ Cell (_____)_____
Address _____

Other _____
Work Phone (_____)_____ Cell (_____)_____
Address _____

Other _____
Work Phone (_____)_____ Cell (_____)_____
Address _____

Other _____
Work Phone (_____)_____ Cell (_____)_____
Address _____

Other _____
Work Phone (_____)_____ Cell (_____)_____
Address _____

Fiduciary Review

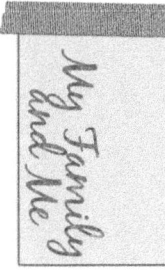

Fiduciary is a term that means: *relating to, or involving a confidence or trust a: held or founded in trust or confidence b: holding in trust*

The people named in your planning documents as fiduciaries are named primarily because you have confidence and trust in them to do the right things and make the right decisions when the time comes.

This is a good time to review the people in your life and in your estate plan to determine if you still want them acting on your behalf. After your review, if you still like your choices, you don't have to do anything. If you want to make changes, call your attorney to get your documents amended as quickly as possible.

Here are a few roles someone may have to perform on your behalf:

1. *Disability Panel Members:* determines whether you are mentally incapacitated.
2. *Disability Trustees:* administers your trust if you are mentally incapacitated.
3. *Health Care Representatives:* makes medical decisions if you cannot.
4. *Financial Representatives:* makes financial decisions if you cannot.
5. *Guardians for your minor children:* raises your children if you cannot.
6. *Death Trustees:* administers your trust after you're gone.
7. *Separate Trust Trustees:* administers your heirs' trusts after you're gone.
8. *Personal Representatives:* represents your estate through the probate process.
9. *Business Managers:* manages your business interests if you cannot.

If you have questions on how these people will work together or the decisions they will be making for you, please call your attorney and have it explained to you! It's important that you understand what each role entails and what rights, duties and responsibilities these people have while serving in that role.

Disability Panel Members named in my Living Trust or my Durable Power of Attorney

_____

_____

_____

Disability Trustees named in my Living Trust

_____

_____

_____

Health Care Representatives in my Health Care Power of Attorney

_____

_____

_____

Financial Representatives named in my Durable Power of Attorney

_____

_____

_____

Guardians of my Minor Children

_____

_____

_____

Death Trustees in my Living Trust or in my Last Will & Testament

_____

_____

_____

Separate Trust Trustees

_____

_____

_____

Personal Representatives named in my Last Will & Testament

_____
_____

Business Managers named in the applicable Planning Documents

_____
_____

Other people I have named to do things if I cannot do them myself:

Name	Task

Fiduciary Review

Estate Plan Review Checklist

We update everything in our lives to keep pace with constant change. We change the oil in our cars. We tune–up our skis. We buy new clothes when we grow into or out of our old ones. We change our cell phones because there's a better model with more options. We upgrade our computers and we regularly update our anti–virus software. Our estate plan is not less important.

Here are some ideas to make sure your estate plan continues to meet your needs and the needs of your family when it's time.

- ❑ Does my plan need to be updated?
    - How long ago did I update my plan?
    - Have my needs and goals changed since then?
    - Have my family circumstances changed since then?
    - Have my financial circumstances changed since then?
    - What laws have changed since then?

- ❑ Do I need to change my helpers?
    - Who determines whether I am mentally incapacitated?
    - Who are my Agents under my Health Care Power of Attorney?
    - Who are my Agents under my Financial Powers of Attorney?
    - Who are my Disability Trustees?
    - Who are my Death Trustees?
    - Who takes care of my minor children if I'm disabled or die?
    - Who is my Personal Representative?
    - Who are my clergy and lay contacts?

- ❑ Who inherits my estate, when, and how much?
    - Who are my named beneficiaries?
      (Spouse, Children, Grandchildren, Charities, Others)
    - How have their circumstances changed since I last updated my plan?
    - Are the current distribution provisions for my beneficiaries still relevant?
    - Do the current distribution provisions for my beneficiaries match my needs and goals to theirs?

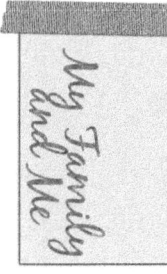

- Are there asset protection possibilities that could enhance my plan for the benefit of my beneficiaries?
- Have tax law changes made my current planning detrimental to my beneficiaries?

❑ Is my plan properly funded?
  - Who is the registered owner of my life insurance?
  - Who is the beneficiary of my life insurance?
  - Who is the primary beneficiary of my retirement plans?
  - Who is the registered owner of my investment accounts and financial assets?
  - Who owns my real estate? Have I recently refinanced any real estate?
  - Have I inadvertently left assets outside of my trust that should be re-titled?
  - Have I left assets out of my trust on purpose?

❑ Are my documents current?
  - Is my trust current with the new tax laws?
  - Are my medical directives and financial power of attorney still valid?
  - What other documents do I need to supplement my plan?
  - Have I left detailed Letters of Instruction to my helpers?

❑ Are my assets properly invested?
  Your investment strategy needs to be reviewed and updated and coordinated with your estate planning strategy. This review should be done with your entire team of advisors: attorneys, tax, insurance, and financial professionals.

❑ Is my insurance adequate for my family's needs and goals?
  Your insurance needs depend on your family's needs and goals. Consider meeting with an insurance professional who will take the time to get to know you and develop an insurance plan based on your needs and goals and one that will be coordinated with your overall financial and estate plan.

❑ Have I reviewed my plan with my immediate helpers?
  Just because you named them as helpers in your estate plan does not mean that they must help. Even if they agreed when you asked them, they can always change their mind when it comes time for them to act. You should regularly review your

plan with your helpers and be prepared to ask and answer some tough questions. Make sure they still want to help and will follow your directions. If your helpers can't, won't, or aren't qualified to work your plan when needed, the plan will fail.

- Are my helpers willing to help?
- Are my helpers qualified to help?
- Do my helpers know where to look for my documents?
- Do my helpers know where to turn for more help?
- Will my helpers continue to work with my advisor team?

Conclusion

A comprehensive, personalized estate plan is vital to protect you and your family from unnecessary expenses, loss of control, disability, and high taxes. It is essential for providing that your unique and individual goals, values, dreams and expectations will be met how you want, when you want, and the way you want.

Good estate planning is an unselfish act of love allowing for a smoother transition for your loved ones when you die or become disabled.

Every estate plan must be reviewed periodically so that it stays current with your intentions and desires. An out-of-date estate plan can be worse than no plan at all.

This checklist is a general guideline and does not constitute specific legal advice regarding any situation, either probate or no probate.

The list includes most items required or advisable when proceeding through probate in many states, but is not presented as all-inclusive of the duties of a personal representative of a will in any particular state.

My Finances and Insurance

Funding Review

Funding is a term that refers to changing the owner and/or beneficiary of an asset to ensure that your estate plan works as it should. Your planning documents cannot control assets that aren't properly titled. For instance, if you own property in joint tenancy with someone, then upon your death the property passes automatically to the other joint tenant irrespective of what your planning documents say.

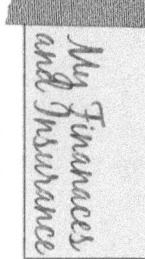

Funding is the process of putting the fuel in the estate planning vehicle. If your assets aren't properly titled or if beneficiaries are not properly named, your planning vehicle is no better than the 2004 Porsche Boxter that sits in your garage because it doesn't have any gasoline. Incomplete funding of your plan may inadvertently give the vehicle's gasoline to someone other than those you intended. For instance, we are working on a probate case now where the deceased person will pass over 45% of his estate outside of his estate plan because of incomplete or inaccurate funding!

This is a good time to review how your assets are titled. In addition, do a quick review of your assets and make sure that everything you own is identified in the Trust Assets tab of your Portfolio. After your review, if you have any questions about how things should be titled, call us and we'll be happy to speak with you about it.

Your loved ones will be forever grateful that you took the time to ensure your estate plan works when you need it most and that it controls ALL of your assets for their benefit.

Real Estate Information

Property Address _____

Name of Owners _____

Date of Purchase _____ Purchase Price _____

Mortgage Held By _____

Address of Mortgage Holder _____

Approximate Mortgage Balance _____ Date _____

Number of Years on Mortgage _____ Interest Rate _____

Loan Number _____ Payment Amount _____

Due Date _____ Late Date _____

Property Taxes _____

Location of Title/Deed _____

Description of Capital Improvements:

_____Date _____ Cost _____

_____Date _____ Cost _____

_____Date _____ Cost _____

_____Date _____ Cost _____

_____Date _____ Cost _____

Other Information _____

_____

_____

_____

_____

_____

_____

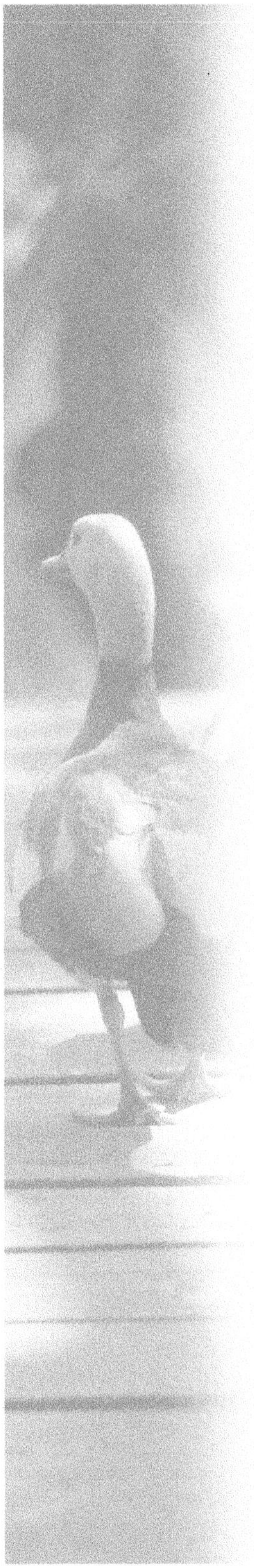

Property Address _____

Name of Owners _____

Date of Purchase _____ Purchase Price _____

Mortgage Held By _____

Address of Mortgage Holder _____

Approximate Mortgage Balance _____ Date _____

Number of Years on Mortgage _____ Interest Rate _____

Loan Number _____ Payment Amount _____

Due Date _____ Late Date _____

Property Taxes _____

Location of Title/Deed _____

Description of Capital Improvements:

_____ Date _____ Cost _____

_____ Date _____ Cost _____

_____ Date _____ Cost _____

_____ Date _____ Cost _____

_____ Date _____ Cost _____

Other Information _____

_____

_____

_____

_____

_____

_____

_____

_____

_____

_____

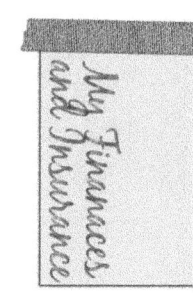

My Finances and Insurance

Property Address _____

Name of Owners _____

Date of Purchase _____ Purchase Price _____

Mortgage Held By _____

Address of Mortgage Holder _____

Approximate Mortgage Balance _____ Date _____

Number of Years on Mortgage _____ Interest Rate _____

Loan Number _____ Payment Amount _____

Due Date _____ Late Date _____

Property Taxes _____

Location of Title/Deed _____

Description of Capital Improvements:

_____ Date _____ Cost _____

_____ Date _____ Cost _____

_____ Date _____ Cost _____

_____ Date _____ Cost _____

_____ Date _____ Cost _____

Other Information _____

_____
_____
_____
_____
_____
_____
_____
_____
_____
_____

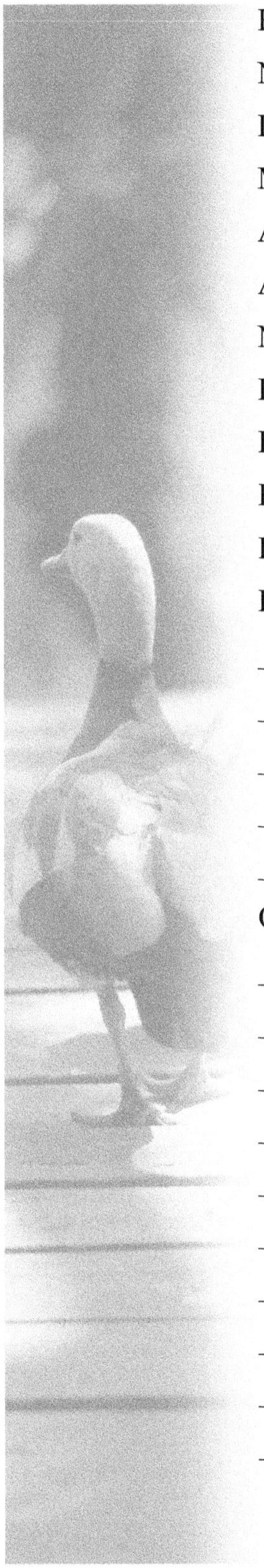

Property Address _____

Name of Owners _____

Date of Purchase _____ Purchase Price _____

Mortgage Held By _____

Address of Mortgage Holder _____

Approximate Mortgage Balance _____ Date _____

Number of Years on Mortgage _____ Interest Rate _____

Loan Number _____ Payment Amount _____

Due Date _____ Late Date _____

Property Taxes _____

Location of Title/Deed _____

Description of Capital Improvements:

_____ Date _____ Cost _____

_____ Date _____ Cost _____

_____ Date _____ Cost _____

_____ Date _____ Cost _____

_____ Date _____ Cost _____

Other Information _____

_____

_____

_____

_____

_____

_____

_____

_____

_____

_____

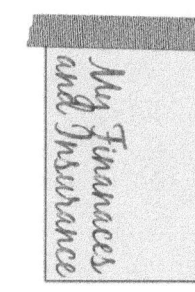

My Finances and Insurance

Real Estate Information

Investment Account Information

Investment Company _____

Account Number _____

Address _____

Phone (_____)_____

Owner

❏ Trust ❏ Joint with _____ ❏ Individual ❏ Custodial

Individual(s) authorized to give instructions on account

Name	Phone
_____	(_____)_____
_____	(_____)_____

Location of important papers regarding account

_____

_____

_____

Details of account

_____

_____

_____

_____

_____

_____

_____

_____

_____

_____

Investment Company _____

Account Number _____

Address _____

Phone (_____) _____

Owner

❏ Trust ❏ Joint with _____ ❏ Individual ❏ Custodial

Individual(s) authorized to give instructions on account

Name	Phone
_____	(___) _____
_____	(___) _____

Location of important papers regarding account

_____
_____
_____

Details of account

_____
_____
_____
_____
_____
_____
_____
_____
_____
_____
_____
_____
_____
_____

Investment Account Information

Investment Company _____

Account Number _____

Address _____

Phone (_____)_____

Owner

❏ Trust ❏ Joint with _____ ❏ Individual ❏ Custodial

Individual(s) authorized to give instructions on account

Name	Phone
_____	(_____)_____
_____	(_____)_____

Location of important papers regarding account

_____

_____

_____

Details of account

_____

_____

_____

_____

_____

_____

_____

_____

_____

_____

_____

_____

_____

_____

Investment Company _____

Account Number _____

Address _____

Phone (_____)_____

Owner

❑ Trust   ❑ Joint with _____ ❑ Individual ❑ Custodial

Individual(s) authorized to give instructions on account

Name   Phone

_____   (_____) _____

_____   (_____) _____

Location of important papers regarding account

_____
_____
_____

Details of account

_____
_____
_____
_____
_____
_____
_____
_____
_____
_____
_____
_____
_____
_____

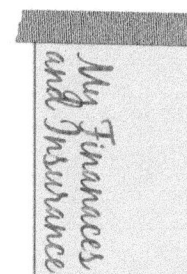
My Finances and Insurance

Investment Account Information

Retirement Plan Information

Name of Plan _____
- ❑ IRA   ❑ Roth IRA   ❑ Inherited IRA   ❑ Rollover IRA
- ❑ 401(k) ❑ 403(b)   ❑ SEP IRA   ❑ SIMPLE IRA
- ❑ Pension ❑ 401(A)   ❑ 412(i)   ❑ _____

Institution Administering Fund _____

Address _____

Phone (_____) _____ Contact _____

Balance _____ As of this date _____

Beneficiaries _____

Location of documents pertaining to fund _____

Other information _____

_____

_____

Name of Plan _____
- ❑ IRA   ❑ Roth IRA   ❑ Inherited IRA   ❑ Rollover IRA
- ❑ 401(k) ❑ 403(b)   ❑ SEP IRA   ❑ SIMPLE IRA
- ❑ Pension ❑ 401(A)   ❑ 412(i)   ❑ _____

Institution Administering Fund _____

Address _____

Phone (_____) _____ Contact _____

Balance _____ As of this date _____

Beneficiaries _____

Location of documents pertaining to fund _____

Other information _____

_____

_____

Name of Plan _____
- ❏ IRA   ❏ Roth IRA   ❏ Inherited IRA   ❏ Rollover IRA
- ❏ 401(k)   ❏ 403(b)   ❏ SEP IRA   ❏ SIMPLE IRA
- ❏ Pension   ❏ 401(A)   ❏ 412(i)   ❏ _____

Institution Administering Fund _____

Address _____

Phone (_____) _____ Contact _____

Balance _____ As of this date _____

Beneficiaries _____

Location of documents pertaining to fund _____

Other information _____

_____

_____

_____

Name of Plan _____
- ❏ IRA   ❏ Roth IRA   ❏ Inherited IRA   ❏ Rollover IRA
- ❏ 401(k)   ❏ 403(b)   ❏ SEP IRA   ❏ SIMPLE IRA
- ❏ Pension   ❏ 401(A)   ❏ 412(i)   ❏ _____

Institution Administering Fund _____

Address _____

Phone (_____) _____ Contact _____

Balance _____ As of this date _____

Beneficiaries _____

Location of documents pertaining to fund _____

Other information _____

_____

_____

_____

Retirement Plan Information

Education Savings Accounts

Type of Plan ❑ 529 ❑ UGMA / UTMA ❑ Coverdell ESA

Owner / Custodian _____

Institution Administering Plan _____

Account Number _____

Address _____

Phone (_____) _____

Contact _____

Balance _____ As of this date _____

Beneficiaries _____

_____

_____

Location of documents pertaining to plan _____

Other information _____

_____
_____
_____
_____
_____
_____
_____
_____
_____
_____
_____
_____
_____

Type of Plan ❏ 529　　❏ UGMA / UTMA　　❏ Coverdell ESA

Owner / Custodian _____

Institution Administering Plan _____

Account Number_____

Address _____

Phone (_____) _____

Contact _____

Balance _____ As of this date _____

Beneficiaries _____

_____

_____

Location of documents pertaining to plan _____

Other information _____

_____

_____

_____

_____

_____

_____

_____

_____

_____

_____

_____

_____

_____

_____

Education Savings Accounts

Type of Plan ☐ 529 ☐ UGMA / UTMA ☐ Coverdell ESA

Owner / Custodian _____

Institution Administering Plan _____

Account Number _____

Address _____

Phone (_____) _____

Contact _____

Balance _____ As of this date _____

Beneficiaries _____

_____

_____

Location of documents pertaining to plan _____

Other information _____

_____

_____

_____

_____

_____

_____

_____

_____

_____

_____

_____

_____

_____

_____

Type of Plan ❑ 529 ❑ UGMA / UTMA ❑ Coverdell ESA

Owner / Custodian _____

Institution Administering Plan _____

Account Number_____

Address _____

Phone (_____) _____

Contact _____

Balance _____ As of this date _____

Beneficiaries _____

_____

_____

Location of documents pertaining to plan _____

Other information _____

_____
_____
_____
_____
_____
_____
_____
_____
_____
_____
_____
_____
_____
_____
_____
_____

My Finances and Insurance

Education Savings Accounts

Annuity Contracts

Annuitant _____

Owner _____

Annuity Type ❑ Fixed ❑ Variable

Insurance Company _____

Address _____

Phone (_____) _____

Contract Number _____

Annuitized ❑ Yes ❑ No

Payment Dates _____

❑ Check ❑ Direct Deposit ❑ Other

Balance _____ As of this date _____

Surrender charges _____

Beneficiaries _____

_____

_____

Location of Policy _____

Details of Coverage _____

_____

_____

_____

_____

_____

_____

_____

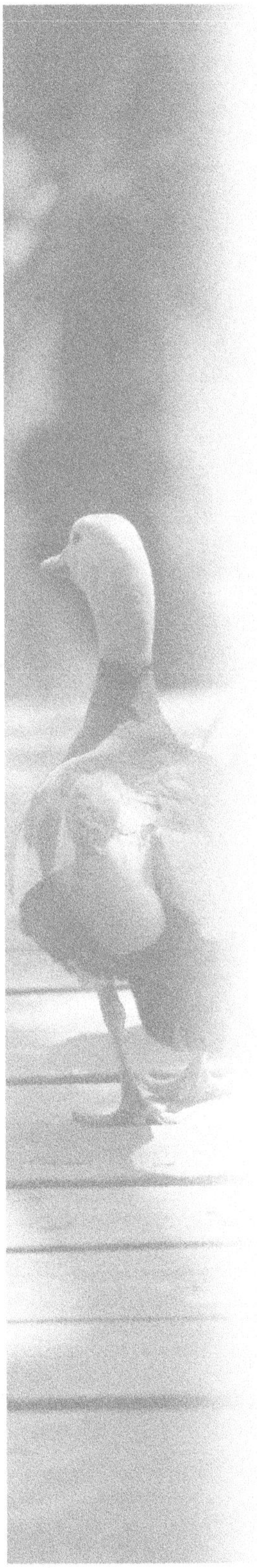

Annuitant _____

Owner _____

Annuity Type ❏ Fixed ❏ Variable

Insurance Company _____

Address _____

Phone (_____) _____

Contract Number _____

Annuitized ❏ Yes ❏ No

Payment Dates _____

❏ Check ❏ Direct Deposit ❏ Other _____

Balance _____ As of this date _____

Surrender charges _____

Beneficiaries _____
_____
_____

Location of Policy _____

Details of Coverage _____
_____
_____
_____
_____
_____
_____
_____
_____
_____
_____
_____
_____

Annuity Contracts

Annuitant _____

Owner _____

Annuity Type ❑ Fixed ❑ Variable

Insurance Company _____

Address _____

Phone (_____) _____

Contract Number _____

Annuitized ❑ Yes ❑ No

Payment Dates _____

❑ Check ❑ Direct Deposit ❑ Other _____

Balance _____ As of this date _____

Surrender charges _____

Beneficiaries _____

_____

_____

Location of Policy _____

Details of Coverage _____

_____

_____

_____

_____

_____

_____

_____

_____

_____

_____

_____

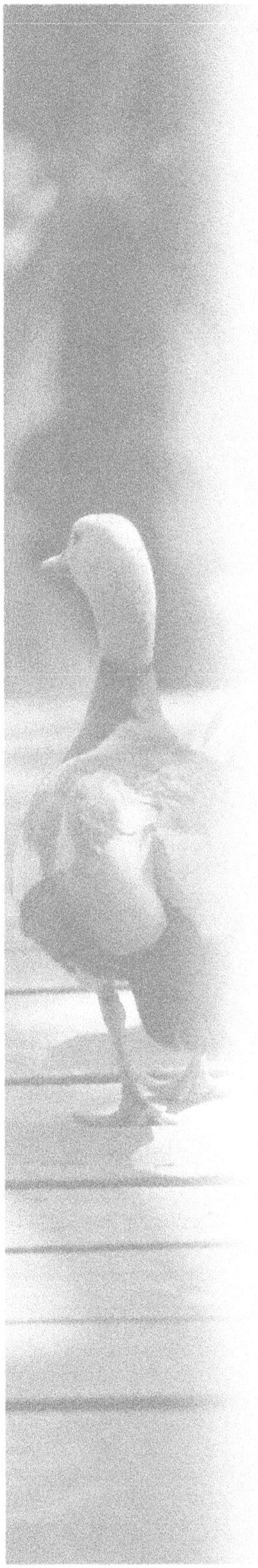

Annuitant _____

Owner _____

Annuity Type ❏ Fixed ❏ Variable

Insurance Company _____

Address _____

Phone (_____) _____

Contract Number _____

Annuitized ❏ Yes ❏ No

Payment Dates _____

❏ Check ❏ Direct Deposit ❏ Other _____

Balance _____ As of this date _____

Surrender charges _____

Beneficiaries _____

_____

_____

Location of Policy _____

Details of Coverage _____

_____

_____

_____

_____

_____

_____

_____

_____

_____

_____

_____

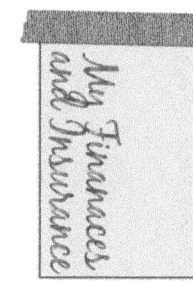

Annuity Contracts

Bank Account Information

Bank _____

Account Number _____

Address _____

Phone (_____)_____

    ❑ Trust   ❑ Joint with _____

    ❑ Individual   ❑ Custodial

    ❑ Checking   ❑ Money Market

    ❑ Savings

Individual(s) authorized to sign on account:

Name	Phone
_____	(_____) _____
_____	(_____) _____

Location of checkbook, check register, or savings passbook:

_____

_____

_____

Notes _____

_____

_____

_____

Bank _____

Account Number _____

Address _____

Phone (_____)_____

    ❏ Trust   ❏ Joint with _____

    ❏ Individual   ❏ Custodial

    ❏ Checking   ❏ Money Market

    ❏ Savings

Individual(s) authorized to sign on account:

Name   Phone

_____   (_____)_____

_____   (_____)_____

Location of checkbook, check register, or savings passbook:

_____

_____

_____

Notes _____

_____

_____

_____

_____

_____

_____

Bank Account Information

Bank _____

Account Number _____

Address _____

Phone (_____)_____

    ❑ Trust   ❑ Joint with _____

    ❑ Individual   ❑ Custodial

    ❑ Checking   ❑ Money Market

    ❑ Savings

Individual(s) authorized to sign on account:

Name	Phone
_____	(_____) _____
_____	(_____) _____

Location of checkbook, check register, or savings passbook:

_____

_____

_____

Notes _____

_____

_____

_____

_____

_____

_____

_____

Bank _____

Account Number _____

Address _____

Phone (_____) _____

- ❏ Trust
- ❏ Individual
- ❏ Checking
- ❏ Savings

- ❏ Joint with _____
- ❏ Custodial
- ❏ Money Market

Individual(s) authorized to sign on account:

Name	Phone
_____	(_____) _____
_____	(_____) _____

Location of checkbook, check register, or savings passbook:

_____
_____
_____

Notes _____
_____
_____
_____
_____
_____
_____

Automobile Information

Make _____ Model _____ Year _____

License Plate Number _____

Date Purchased _____

Registered Owner _____

Seller _____

Address _____

Loan carried by _____

Address _____

Title Number _____ Location of Title _____

Notes _____

_____

_____

Make _____ Model _____ Year _____

License Plate Number _____

Date Purchased _____

Registered Owner _____

Seller _____

Address _____

Loan carried by _____

Address _____

Title Number _____ Location of Title _____

Notes _____

_____

_____

Make _____ Model _____ Year _____

License Plate Number _____

Date Purchased _____

Registered Owner _____

Seller _____

Address _____

Loan carried by _____

Address _____

Title Number _____ Location of Title _____

Notes _____

_____

_____

_____

Make _____ Model _____ Year _____

License Plate Number _____

Date Purchased _____

Registered Owner _____

Seller _____

Address _____

Loan carried by _____

Address _____

Title Number _____ Location of Title _____

Notes _____

_____

_____

_____

Automobile Information

Make _____ Model _____ Year _____

License Plate Number _____

Date Purchased _____

Registered Owner _____

Seller _____

Address _____

Loan carried by _____

Address _____

Title Number _____ Location of Title _____

Notes _____

_____

_____

_____

Make _____ Model _____ Year _____

License Plate Number _____

Date Purchased _____

Registered Owner _____

Seller _____

Address _____

Loan carried by _____

Address _____

Title Number _____ Location of Title _____

Notes _____

_____

_____

_____

Make _____ Model _____ Year _____

License Plate Number _____

Date Purchased _____

Registered Owner _____

Seller _____

Address _____

Loan carried by _____

Address _____

Title Number _____ Location of Title _____

Notes _____

_____

_____

_____

Make _____ Model _____ Year _____

License Plate Number _____

Date Purchased _____

Registered Owner _____

Seller _____

Address _____

Loan carried by _____

Address _____

Title Number _____ Location of Title _____

Notes _____

_____

_____

_____

Automobile Information

Business Information

Business Name _____

❑ Sole Proprietorship ❑ Partnership ❑ Corporation

Owner

Name _____

Address _____

Phone (_____)_____

Owner

Name _____

Address _____

Phone (_____)_____

Attorney

Name _____

Address _____

Phone (_____)_____

Accountant

Name _____

Address _____

Phone (_____)_____

Bank Accounts

Contact _____ Account # _____

Bank _____

Address _____

Phone (_____)_____

Contact _____ Account # _____

Bank _____

Address _____

Phone (_____)_____

Location of Business Records _____

_____

_____

_____

Other Important Business Information_____

_____

_____

_____

_____

_____

_____

_____

_____

_____

_____

_____

_____

_____

_____

_____

Business Information

Business Name _____

☐ Sole Proprietorship   ☐ Partnership   ☐ Corporation

Owner

Name _____

Address _____

Phone (_____) _____

Owner

Name _____

Address _____

Phone (_____) _____

Attorney

Name _____

Address _____

Phone (_____) _____

Accountant

Name _____

Address _____

Phone (_____) _____

Bank Accounts

Contact _____ Account # _____

Bank _____

Address _____

Phone (_____) _____

Contact _____ Account # _____

Bank _____

Address _____

Phone (_____) _____

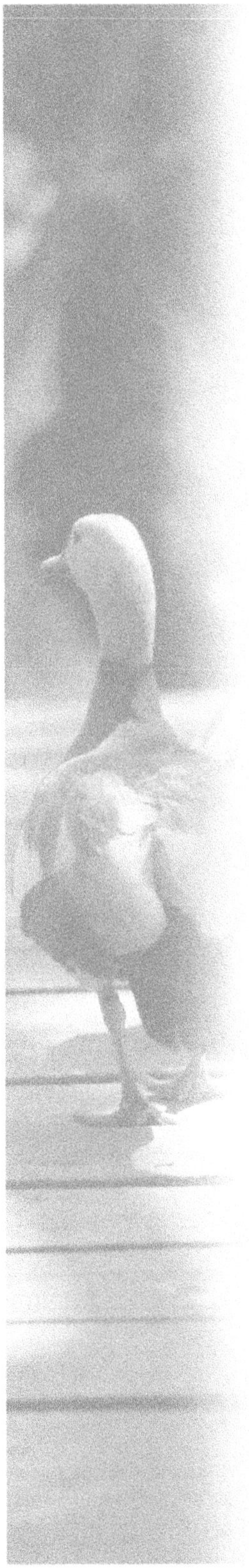

Location of Business Records ____________________

Other Important Business Information____________________

My Finances and Insurance

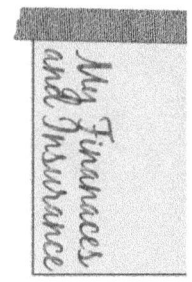

Business Name _____

❑ Sole Proprietorship ❑ Partnership ❑ Corporation

Owner

Name _____

Address _____

Phone (_____)_____

Owner

Name _____

Address _____

Phone (_____)_____

Attorney

Name _____

Address _____

Phone (_____)_____

Accountant

Name _____

Address _____

Phone (_____)_____

Bank Accounts

Contact _____ Account # _____

Bank _____

Address _____

Phone (_____)_____

Contact _____ Account # _____

Bank _____

Address _____

Phone (_____)_____

Location of Business Records _____

_____
_____
_____

Other Important Business Information _____

_____
_____
_____
_____
_____
_____
_____
_____
_____
_____
_____
_____
_____
_____
_____
_____
_____
_____
_____

My Finances and Insurance

Personal Property

Description of Property

_____

_____

_____

_____

Owners _____

_____

Property Detail

Date Purchased _____

Date of Last Appraisal _____

_____

Appraised Value _____

Location of Records _____

_____

_____

_____

_____

Notes _____

_____

_____

_____

_____

_____

Description of Property

_____
_____
_____
_____

Owners _____
_____

Property Detail

Date Purchased _____
Date of Last Appraisal _____
_____

Appraised Value _____
Location of Records _____
_____
_____
_____
_____

Notes _____
_____
_____
_____
_____
_____
_____
_____

Description of Property

_____
_____
_____
_____

Owners _____
_____

Property Detail

Date Purchased _____
Date of Last Appraisal _____
_____
Appraised Value _____
Location of Records_____
_____
_____
_____
_____

Notes _____
_____
_____
_____
_____
_____
_____
_____
_____

Description of Property

_____
_____
_____
_____

Owners _____
_____

Property Detail

Date Purchased _____

Date of Last Appraisal _____
_____

Appraised Value _____

Location of Records _____
_____
_____
_____
_____

Notes _____
_____
_____
_____
_____
_____
_____
_____

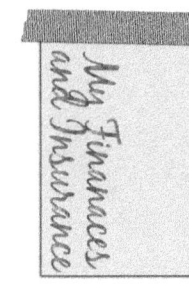

My Finances and Insurance

Safe Deposit Box

Box Location _____

Address _____

_____

Box Number _____ Key Location _____

Phone (_____)_____ Fax (_____)_____

Website _____

Persons authorized to access box

_____   _____

_____   _____

_____   _____

Safe deposit box contents

_____

_____

_____

_____

_____

_____

_____

_____

Notes

_____

_____

_____

_____

Box Location _____

Address _____

_____

Box Number _____ Key Location _____

Phone (_____)_____ Fax (_____)_____

Website _____

Persons authorized to access box

_____   _____

_____   _____

_____

Safe deposit box contents

_____

_____

_____

_____

_____

_____

_____

_____

Notes

_____

_____

_____

_____

_____

_____

Safe Deposit Box

Internet Account Access

Name _____

    Web Address _____

    Account Number _____

    Logon / Username _____

    Password _____

Name _____

    Web Address _____

    Account Number _____

    Logon / Username _____

    Password _____

Name _____

    Web Address _____

    Account Number _____

    Logon / Username _____

    Password _____

Name _____

    Web Address _____

    Account Number _____

    Logon / Username _____

    Password _____

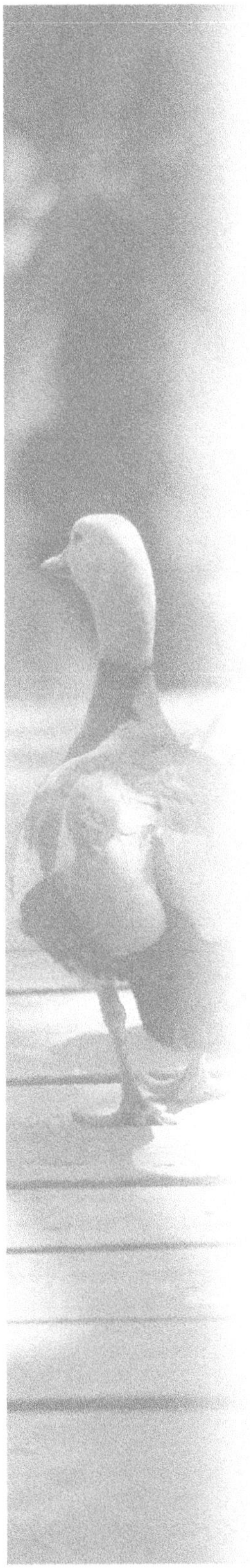

Name _____

    Web Address _____

    Account Number _____

    Logon / Username _____

    Password _____

Name _____

    Web Address _____

    Account Number _____

    Logon / Username _____

    Password _____

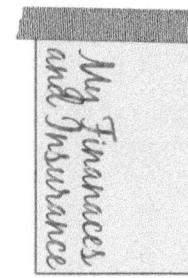

My Finances and Insurance

Name _____

    Web Address _____

    Account Number _____

    Logon / Username _____

    Password _____

Name _____

    Web Address _____

    Account Number _____

    Logon / Username _____

    Password _____

Name _____

    Web Address _____

    Account Number _____

    Logon / Username _____

    Password _____

Internet Account Access

Name _____

    Web Address _____

    Account Number _____

    Logon / Username _____

    Password _____

Name _____

    Web Address _____

    Account Number _____

    Logon / Username _____

    Password _____

Name _____

    Web Address _____

    Account Number _____

    Logon / Username _____

    Password _____

Name _____

    Web Address _____

    Account Number _____

    Logon / Username _____

    Password _____

Name _____

    Web Address _____

    Account Number _____

    Logon / Username _____

    Password _____

Notes

Credit Card Information

Card Issued By _____

Phone (_____)_____ PIN _____

Card Number _____

Expiration Date _____ Security Code _____

It is a: ❏ MasterCard ❏ Visa ❏ Discover ❏ American Express

Location of Card _____

Individuals authorized to sign on card _____

Is there any insurance to pay off this balance?_____

Card Issued By _____

Phone (_____)_____ PIN _____

Card Number _____

Expiration Date _____ Security Code _____

It is a: ❏ MasterCard ❏ Visa ❏ Discover ❏ American Express

Location of Card _____

Individuals authorized to sign on card _____

Is there any insurance to pay off this balance?_____

Card Issued By _____

Phone (_____)_____ PIN _____

Card Number _____

Expiration Date _____ Security Code _____

It is a: ❏ MasterCard ❏ Visa ❏ Discover ❏ American Express

Location of Card _____

Individuals authorized to sign on card _____

Is there any insurance to pay off this balance?_____

Card Issued By _____

Phone (_____)_____ PIN _____

Card Number _____

Expiration Date _____ Security Code _____

It is a: ❑ MasterCard ❑ Visa ❑ Discover ❑ American Express

Location of Card _____

Individuals authorized to sign on card _____

Is there any insurance to pay off this balance?_____

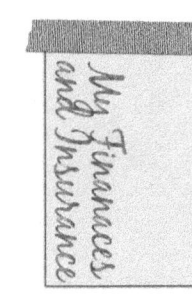

Card Issued By _____

Phone (_____)_____ PIN _____

Card Number _____

Expiration Date _____ Security Code _____

It is a: ❑ MasterCard ❑ Visa ❑ Discover ❑ American Express

Location of Card _____

Individuals authorized to sign on card _____

Is there any insurance to pay off this balance?_____

Card Issued By _____

Phone (_____)_____ PIN _____

Card Number _____

Expiration Date _____ Security Code _____

It is a: ❑ MasterCard ❑ Visa ❑ Discover ❑ American Express

Location of Card _____

Individuals authorized to sign on card _____

Is there any insurance to pay off this balance?_____

Credit Card Information

Card Issued By _____
Phone (_____)_____ PIN _____
Card Number _____
Expiration Date _____ Security Code _____
It is a: ❏ MasterCard ❏ Visa ❏ Discover ❏ American Express
Location of Card _____
Individuals authorized to sign on card _____
Is there any insurance to pay off this balance?_____

Card Issued By _____
Phone (_____)_____ PIN _____
Card Number _____
Expiration Date _____ Security Code _____
It is a: ❏ MasterCard ❏ Visa ❏ Discover ❏ American Express
Location of Card _____
Individuals authorized to sign on card _____
Is there any insurance to pay off this balance?_____

Card Issued By _____
Phone (_____)_____ PIN _____
Card Number _____
Expiration Date _____ Security Code _____
It is a: ❏ MasterCard ❏ Visa ❏ Discover ❏ American Express
Location of Card _____
Individuals authorized to sign on card _____
Is there any insurance to pay off this balance?_____

Other Loan Information

(For loans not covered in earlier sections)

Lender _____

Address _____

Phone (____) _____

Amount of Loan _____ Payment Amount _____

Due Date _____ Date loan is paid off _____

Type of Loan _____

Location of loan paperwork _____

Other information _____

_____

_____

_____

Lender _____

Address _____

Phone (____) _____

Amount of Loan _____ Payment Amount _____

Due Date _____ Date loan is paid off _____

Type of Loan _____

Location of loan paperwork _____

Other information _____

_____

_____

_____

_____

Lender _____
Address _____
Phone (____) _____
Amount of Loan _____ Payment Amount _____
Due Date _____ Date loan is paid off _____
Type of Loan _____
Location of loan paperwork _____
Other information _____
_____
_____
_____
_____
_____

Lender _____
Address _____
Phone (____) _____
Amount of Loan _____ Payment Amount _____
Due Date _____ Date loan is paid off _____
Type of Loan _____
Location of loan paperwork _____
Other information _____
_____
_____
_____
_____
_____

Life Insurance

Owner _____ Insured _____

Death Benefit _____

Policy Type

    ❑ ____ Year Term   ❑ Whole Life   ❑ Universal

    ❑ Variable Universal   ❑ Rider _____

Insurance Company _____

Address _____

Phone (_____) _____ Agent's Name _____

Policy Number _____ Premium Amount _____

Due Dates _____ ❑ Bank Draft ❑ Check ❑ Other

Location of Policy _____

Beneficiaries _____

_____

Details of Coverage _____

_____

_____

_____

_____

Notes _____

_____

_____

_____

_____

Disability Insurance Information

Owner _____ Insured _____

Death Benefit _____

Policy Type

    ❏ _____ Year Term   ❏ Whole Life   ❏ Universal

    ❏ Variable Universal   ❏ Rider _____

Insurance Company _____

Address _____

Phone (_____) _____ Agent's Name _____

Policy Number _____ Premium Amount _____

Due Dates _____ ❏ Bank Draft ❏ Check ❏ Other

Location of Policy _____

Beneficiaries _____

_____

Details of Coverage _____

_____

_____

_____

_____

_____

Notes _____

_____

_____

_____

_____

_____

_____

Owner _____ Insured _____

Death Benefit _____

Policy Type

 ❏ ____ Year Term ❏ Whole Life ❏ Universal

 ❏ Variable Universal ❏ Rider _____

Insurance Company _____

Address _____

Phone (____) _____ Agent's Name _____

Policy Number _____ Premium Amount _____

Due Dates _____ ❏ Bank Draft ❏ Check ❏ Other

Location of Policy _____

Beneficiaries _____

_____

Details of Coverage _____

_____
_____
_____
_____
_____

Notes _____

_____
_____
_____
_____
_____
_____
_____

My Finances and Insurance

Disability Insurance Information

Owner _____ Insured _____

Death Benefit _____

Policy Type

  ❏ _____ Year Term ❏ Whole Life ❏ Universal

  ❏ Variable Universal ❏ Rider _____

Insurance Company _____

Address _____

Phone (_____) _____ Agent's Name _____

Policy Number _____ Premium Amount _____

Due Dates _____ ❏ Bank Draft ❏ Check ❏ Other

Location of Policy _____

Beneficiaries _____

_____

Details of Coverage _____

_____

_____

_____

_____

Notes _____

_____

_____

_____

_____

_____

_____

Health and Major Medical Insurance

Individuals Covered by Policy:

_____   _____

_____   _____

Company _____

Address _____

Phone (_____) _____ Agent's name _____

Policy Number _____

Deductible _____ Premium Amount _____

Due Dates _____ ☐ Bank Draft ☐ Check ☐ Other

Location of Policy _____

Details of Coverage _____

_____

_____

_____

_____

_____

_____

_____

Notes _____

_____

_____

Disability Insurance Information

Individuals Covered by Policy:

_____   _____

_____   _____

Company _____

Address _____

Phone (_____) _____ Agent's name _____

Policy Number _____

Deductible _____ Premium Amount _____

Due Dates _____ ☐ Bank Draft   ☐ Check   ☐ Other

Location of Policy _____

Details of Coverage _____

_____

_____

_____

_____

_____

_____

_____

Notes _____

_____

_____

_____

_____

_____

_____

Disability Insurance Information

Insured _____

Amount _____

Elimination Period _____

Illness _____ Accident _____

Company _____

Address _____

Phone: (_____) _____ Agent's Name _____

Policy Number _____ Premium Amount _____

Due Dates _____ ☐ Bank Draft ☐ Check ☐ Other

Location of Policy _____

Details of Coverage _____

_____

_____

_____

_____

_____

_____

_____

Notes _____

_____

_____

_____

_____

My Finances and Insurance

Insured _____
Amount _____
Elimination Period _____
Illness _____ Accident _____
Company _____
Address _____
Phone: (_____) _____ Agent's Name _____
Policy Number _____ Premium Amount _____
Due Dates _____ ☐ Bank Draft ☐ Check ☐ Other
Location of Policy _____
Details of Coverage _____
_____
_____
_____
_____
_____
_____
_____
_____
_____
_____

Notes _____
_____
_____
_____
_____
_____
_____

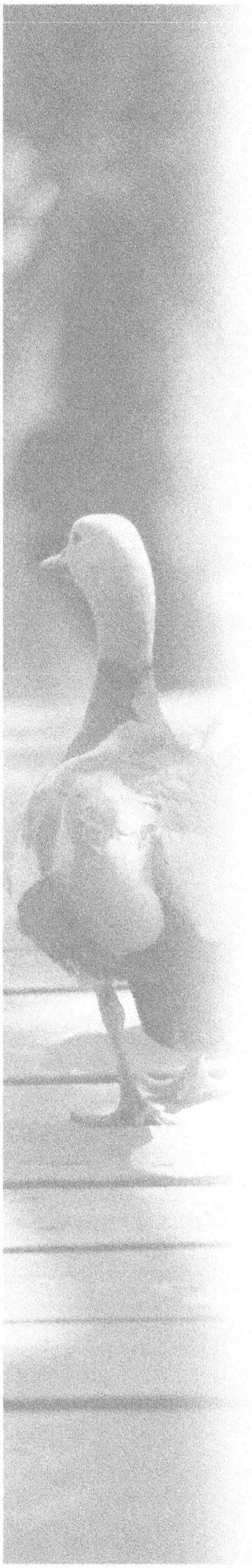

Insured _____

Amount _____

Elimination Period _____

Illness _____ Accident _____

Company _____

Address _____

Phone: (_____) _____ Agent's Name _____

Policy Number _____ Premium Amount _____

Due Dates _____ ☐ Bank Draft ☐ Check ☐ Other

Location of Policy _____

Details of Coverage _____

_____
_____
_____
_____
_____
_____
_____
_____

Notes _____

_____
_____
_____
_____
_____
_____

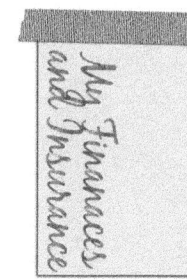
My Finances and Insurance

Disability Insurance Information

Insured _____

Amount _____

Elimination Period _____

Illness _____ Accident _____

Company _____

Address _____

Phone: (_____) _____ Agent's Name _____

Policy Number _____ Premium Amount _____

Due Dates _____ ☐ Bank Draft ☐ Check ☐ Other

Location of Policy _____

Details of Coverage _____

_____

_____

_____

_____

_____

_____

_____

_____

_____

Notes _____

_____

_____

_____

_____

_____

Property Insurance

Property _____

Insurance Company _____

Address _____

Phone (_____) _____ Agent's Name _____

Policy Number _____ Premium Amount _____

Amount _____ ☐ Bank Draft ☐ Check ☐ Other

Amount of Coverage _____ Deductible _____

Location of Policy _____

Details of Coverage _____

_____

_____

_____

Property _____

Insurance Company _____

Address _____

Phone (_____) _____ Agent's Name _____

Policy Number _____ Premium Amount _____

Amount _____ ☐ Bank Draft ☐ Check ☐ Other

Amount of Coverage _____ Deductible _____

Location of Policy _____

Details of Coverage _____

_____

_____

_____

Property _____

Insurance Company _____

Address _____

Phone (_____) _____ Agent's Name _____

Policy Number _____ Premium Amount _____

Amount _____ ☐ Bank Draft ☐ Check ☐ Other

Amount of Coverage _____ Deductible _____

Location of Policy _____

Details of Coverage _____

_____

_____

_____

_____

Property _____

Insurance Company _____

Address _____

Phone (_____) _____ Agent's Name _____

Policy Number _____ Premium Amount _____

Amount _____ ☐ Bank Draft ☐ Check ☐ Other

Amount of Coverage _____ Deductible _____

Location of Policy _____

Details of Coverage _____

_____

_____

_____

_____

Automobile Insurance

Family Licensed Drivers

Name   State / License Number

_____   _____

_____   _____

_____   _____

_____   _____

_____   _____

_____   _____

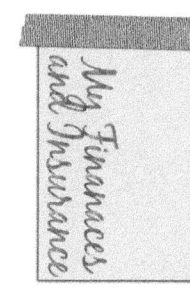

Auto Covered _____

Agent's Name _____

Type of Coverage _____ Deductible _____

Company _____

Address _____ Phone (_____) _____

Policy Number _____ Premium Amount _____

Due Dates _____ ☐ Bank Draft ☐ Check ☐ Other

Location of Policy _____

Details of Coverage _____

_____

Notes _____

_____

_____

_____

_____

_____

Auto Covered _____

Agent's Name _____

Type of Coverage _____ Deductible _____

Company _____

Address _____ Phone (____) _____

Policy Number _____ Premium Amount _____

Due Dates _____ ☐ Bank Draft ☐ Check ☐ Other

Location of Policy _____

Details of Coverage _____

_____

Notes _____

_____

_____

Auto Covered _____

Agent's Name _____

Type of Coverage _____ Deductible _____

Company _____

Address _____ Phone (____) _____

Policy Number _____ Premium Amount _____

Due Dates _____ ☐ Bank Draft ☐ Check ☐ Other

Location of Policy _____

Details of Coverage _____

_____

Notes _____

_____

_____

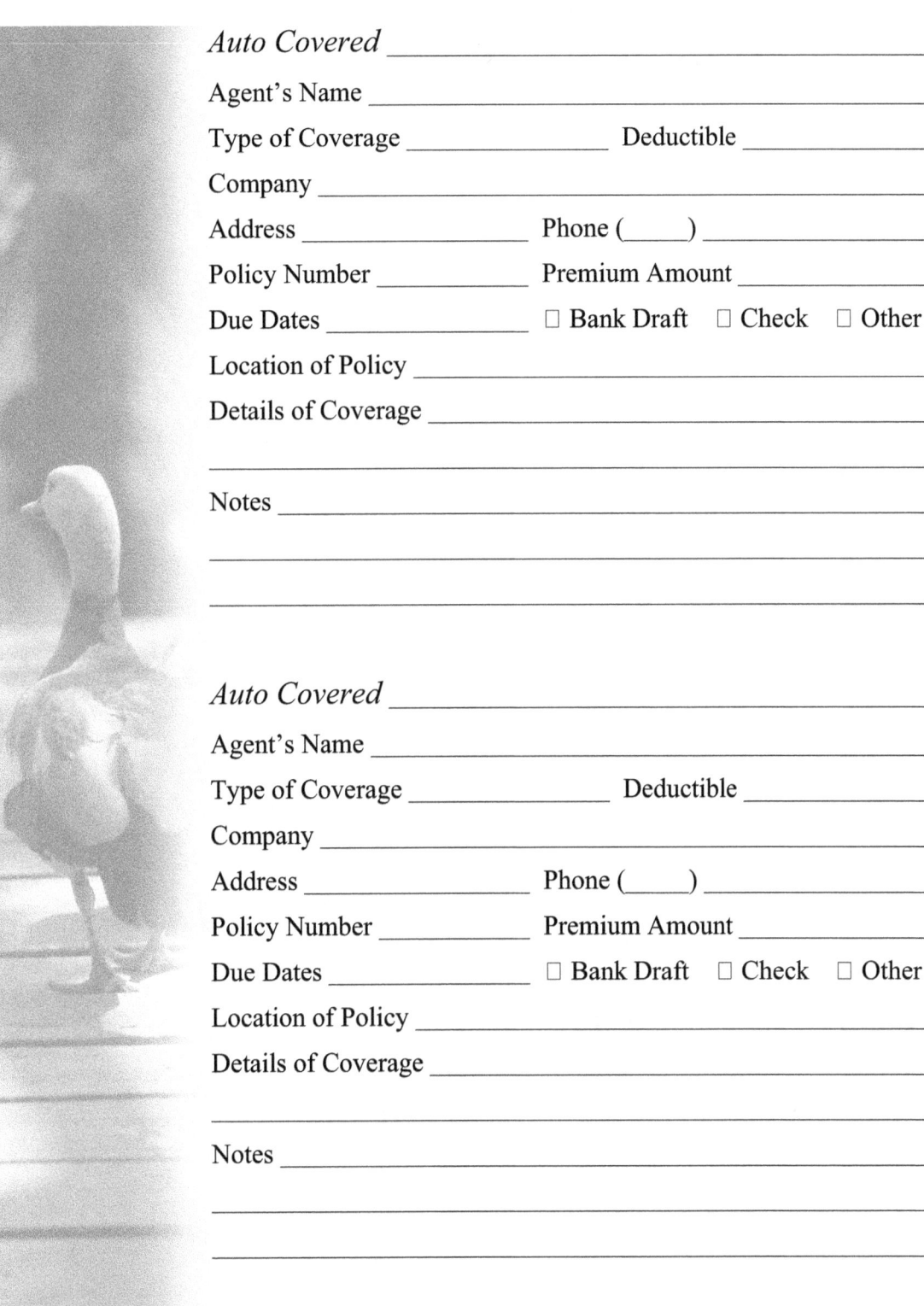

Auto Covered _____

Agent's Name _____

Type of Coverage _____ Deductible _____

Company _____

Address _____ Phone (___) _____

Policy Number _____ Premium Amount _____

Due Dates _____ ☐ Bank Draft ☐ Check ☐ Other

Location of Policy _____

Details of Coverage _____

_____

Notes _____

_____

_____

Auto Covered _____

Agent's Name _____

Type of Coverage _____ Deductible _____

Company _____

Address _____ Phone (___) _____

Policy Number _____ Premium Amount _____

Due Dates _____ ☐ Bank Draft ☐ Check ☐ Other

Location of Policy _____

Details of Coverage _____

_____

Notes _____

_____

_____

Automobile Insurance

Other Insurances

Type of Insurance _____

Insured _____

Company _____

Amount _____

Address _____

Agent's Name _____

Phone (_____) _____ Policy Number _____

Premium Amount _____ Due Dates _____

Amount _____ ❏ Bank Draft ❏ Check ❏ Other

Location of Policy _____

Details of Coverage _____

_____

Type of Insurance _____

Insured _____

Company _____

Amount _____

Address _____

Agent's Name _____

Phone (_____) _____ Policy Number _____

Premium Amount _____ Due Dates _____

Amount _____ ❏ Bank Draft ❏ Check ❏ Other

Location of Policy _____

Details of Coverage _____

_____

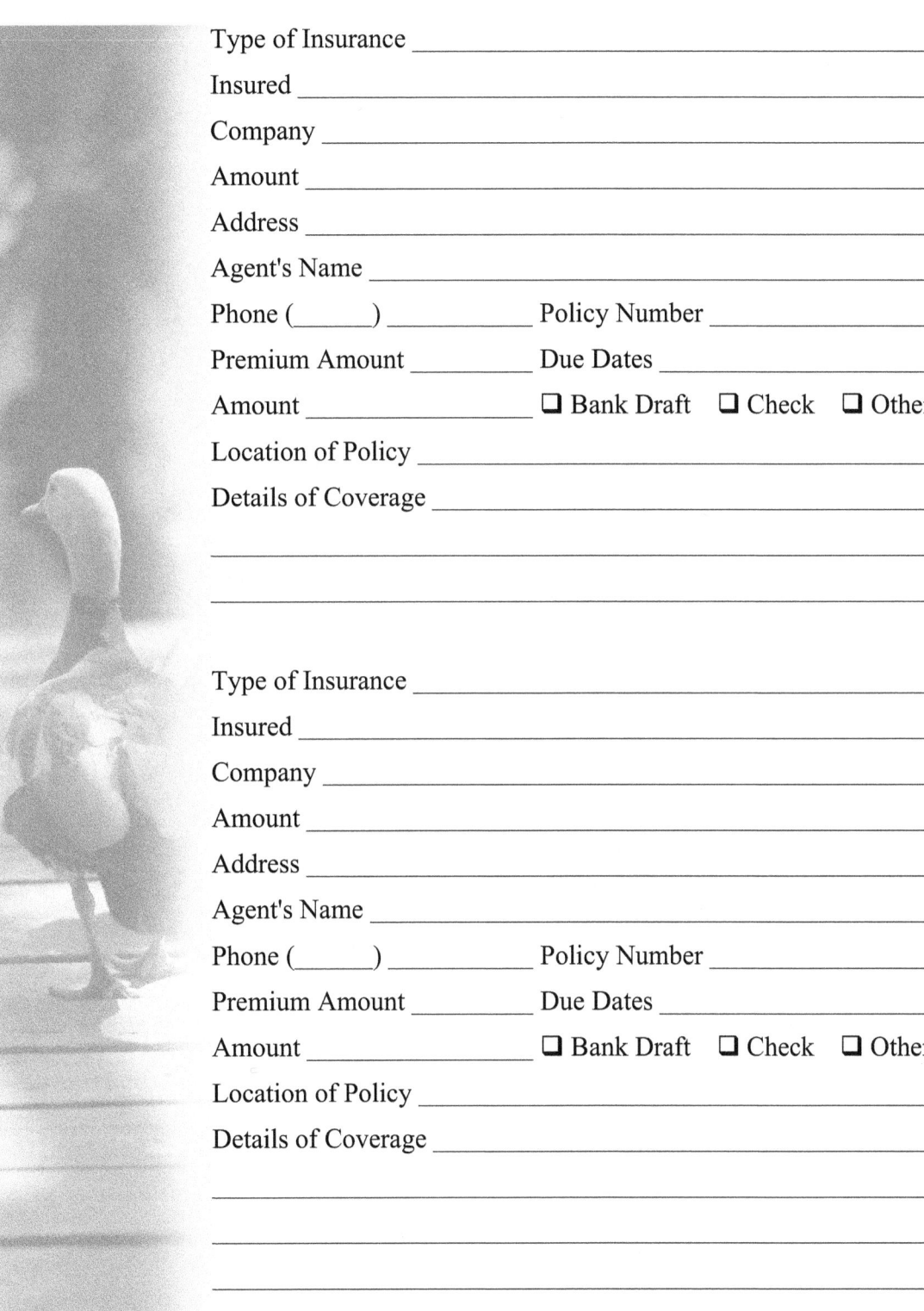

Type of Insurance _____

Insured _____

Company _____

Amount _____

Address _____

Agent's Name _____

Phone (_____) _____ Policy Number _____

Premium Amount _____ Due Dates _____

Amount _____ ❑ Bank Draft ❑ Check ❑ Other

Location of Policy _____

Details of Coverage _____

_____

_____

Type of Insurance _____

Insured _____

Company _____

Amount _____

Address _____

Agent's Name _____

Phone (_____) _____ Policy Number _____

Premium Amount _____ Due Dates _____

Amount _____ ❑ Bank Draft ❑ Check ❑ Other

Location of Policy _____

Details of Coverage _____

_____

_____

_____

Other Insurances

Getting My Ducks In A Row

If I'm Disabled

Disability Guidelines

In designing their estate plans, many people wish to maintain control of their health care throughout their lifetimes. Should they become unable to communicate their wishes due to illness or disability, they want to rely on loved ones and medical professionals to act with their interests in mind. Unfortunately most of us are able to do little more than state our wishes in vague and general terms such as, "I want to avoid 'heroic measures' or 'life-prolonging' procedures."

The objective here is to help you design decision-making guidelines regarding your health care. The goal is to prepare you and your loved ones for any difficult situations that may lie ahead. To that end, the accompanying medical treatment preference materials are for you to discuss with your family and physician.

To ensure that you communicate your wishes as clearly as possible, you should use the enclosed checklist to discuss health care preferences with your personal physician. You should consult your physician and gain his or her insights regarding these issues. Your physician can explain medical terms and options in greater detail and, thus, help you articulate your preferences regarding treatment and/or no treatment.

Also included are four hypothetical medical scenarios for you to consider, discuss with your physician, and declare your wishes. These scenarios assume that you are unable to communicate your preferences or give consent. A simple grid is provided for you to indicate your wishes for each scenario. Register your preferences by initializing the options that best correspond with your wishes.

To eliminate any ambiguity regarding these serious matters, please make certain you record a preferred course of action for each medical treatment/procedure. We hope these materials will facilitate greater communication among you, your loved ones and your physician. In this way you can rest assured that your health care preferences are known should incapacity prevent you from giving direction or consent.

Disability Instructions & Guidelines

During any period I am disabled, I desire that my Trustee consider any written instructions or guidelines dated and signed by me regarding my care. I do hereby give the following instructions for that purpose. My initials next to the particular paragraph indicate my desires.

Initials

_____ It is my desire to remain in my residence as long as possible, even if my mental or physical condition is such that I can no longer provide for myself, please hire companions, nurses, or others necessary to provide for my needs.

_____ If due to my mental, financial, or physical condition it is no longer practical for me to live in my current residence, then it is my desire that a more suitable residence be provided for me.

_____ If it should become necessary for me to enter any hospice, nursing home, retirement center, convalescent home or similar establishment, it is my desire that the level of care provided be consistent with maintaining my maximum degree of independence.

_____ Please consult with my Health Care Representatives appointed under my Health Care Power of Attorney regarding the appropriate balance between quality of care and living arrangements and economic reality.

_____ I want to be provided opportunities to engage in social, recreational and sports activities, including travel, as my health permits. Such decisions shall be made after consultation with my Health Care Representative.

_____ I further direct my Trustee to provide me with books, tapes and similar materials consistent with my interests.

_____ I desire pledges and gifts regularly made to charitable organizations described in Section 170 (c) of the Internal Revenue Code be continued even when I am disabled.

_____ It is my desire to provide for the presence and involvement in my care of religious clergy or spiritual leaders. Please provide them access to me at all times, maintain my memberships in religious or spiritual organizations, and enhance my opportunities to derive comfort and spiritual satisfaction from such activities including religious books, tapes and other materials.

_____ Please provide companionship for me consistent with my needs and preferences. I consider such continuing interaction to be essential.

_____ I don't want any of my assets spent on medical treatment considered "extraordinary" or "heroic" by my Health Care Representative. The decision as to whether treatment shall be considered extraordinary or heroic shall be in the sole and absolute discretion of my Health Care Representative, as guided by the instructions contained in my Health Care Power of Attorney.

_____ I authorize my Health Care Representative, to make any pre-need arrangements considered necessary.

_____ I desire the following additional arrangements regarding my disability:

_____

_____

_____

_____

Printed Name: _____

Signature: _____

Dated: _____

Letter of Instruction to My Health Care Representative

In order to assist my Health Care Representative in making health care decisions for me as comfortably and confidently as possible, I am leaving these specific instructions to be incorporated by reference into the terms of my Durable Medical Power of Attorney.

Family

Initials

_____ I have named the person identified in my Health Care Power of Attorney as my sole Health Care Representative on advice of attorney. The intent of this action was to send one clear signal to my health care providers regarding my wishes, and to avoid even the appearance of conflict among my family and others concerned with my health care.

_____ I do not wish the appointment of the successor agents named in my Health Care Power of Attorney to be perceived as an expression of distrust or a lesser level of confidence in other family members. In fact, I hereby direct each of my Agents to consult, to the fullest extent possible, with all members of my immediate family regarding my health care decisions, particularly those concerning the withholding or withdrawal of treatment should I be in a terminal or irreversible condition.

_____ I direct my Health Care Representative to consult, to the fullest extent possible, with all members of my immediate family regarding any decisions made on my behalf during an emergency health care situation.

_____ I direct my Health Care Representative to hold a conference with all willing and interested members of my immediate family prior to making any decision regarding termination of artificial life support treatments.

_____ I direct my Health Care Representative to consult with the following persons regarding any decisions made on my behalf during an emergency health care situation:

Outsiders
Initials

_____ I have carefully selected the individuals I wish to make medical decisions for me in the event of my incapacity. It is my firm belief that these individuals are best positioned to make such decisions on my behalf. I wish to state emphatically that I do not wish to have other individuals or organizations involved in my health care decision making.

_____ I urge my Health Care Representative to consult the following individuals regarding termination of artificial life support treatments.

❑ Religious Clergy: _____

❑ Medical Professional: _____

❑ Trusted Friend: _____

❑ Other: _____

_____ I consider my health care a personal and private matter, and to the fullest extent possible under the law I urge and request that there be no guardianship or other court intervention in my health care decision making.

Medical Records
Initials

_____ I encourage my Health Care Representative to obtain and use my medical records during any time when my Health Care Representative is making medical decisions for me.

Letter of Instruction to My Health Care Representative

_____ I specifically authorize and direct my attending physicians, hospitals, or other health care providers to give my Health Care Representative the same access to my medical records and the same assistance in understanding my medical records as they would have given me.

_____ I authorize and encourage my Health Care Representative to take my medical records to another physician to get a second opinion before making a medical decision for me.

_____ I encourage my Health Care Representative to share the information in my medical records with all the members of my immediate family.

_____ I am concerned about privacy. I direct my Health Care Representative not to show my medical records to other family members or third parties.

_____ Other medical record concerns:

_____
_____
_____

Choice of Doctors

Initials

_____ I prefer my medical treatment continue with my primary care physician for as long as possible. I direct my Health Care Representative to maintain this relationship.

_____ If my primary care physician is unable to continue my medical treatment for any reason, I request my Health Care Representative consult with my primary care physician to obtain a referral for a quality physician in the same locality, if possible.

_____ If my primary care physician is unable to continue my medical treatment for any reason and cannot refer another quality physician, I direct my Health Care Representative to obtain quality medical care for me. If my Health Care Representative is in doubt about whom to select for my medical care provider, I request that my Health Care Representative seek treatment for me, whenever economically feasible, with a specialist in the area of my medical condition.

_____ I have placed complete trust in my Health Care Representative in both the hiring and termination of a physician. I ask my Health Care Representative to exercise the same diligence in this matter, as he or she would do for his or her own children, spouse or other family members.

_____ Other choice of doctor concerns:

_____

_____

_____

Health Care Facility Preference: Home Care

Initials

_____ My preference is to maintain my current independent lifestyle for as long as possible.

_____ When I can no longer lead an independent lifestyle, my first choice is to remain in my home. However, I realize there may come a time when my desire to remain in my home may burden my loved ones' lives.

_____ I encourage my Health Care Representative to investigate and obtain home-assistance services from any or all of the following organizations: Visiting Nurses Association, Home Hospice Health Care, Meals-On-Wheels, and any other group which provides home-assistance services.

Letter of Instruction to My Health Care Representative

_____ During any time I need home assistance, I request my Health Care Representative determine if a member of my family is able and willing to reside with me and provide the services necessary for me to remain in my home.

_____ When a family member resides with me and provides the services necessary for me to remain in my home, I direct that no room or board fees be charged.

_____ When a family member resides with me and provides the services necessary for me to remain in my home, I direct, upon request in writing to my Health Care Representative by this family member, that my Representative submit a reasonable compensation request to the Trustee of my living trust as a health care expense.

_____ During any time when a family member resides with me and provides the services necessary for me to remain in my home, I direct my Health Care Representative visit my home at least weekly to determine that the level of care I am receiving is appropriate.

Family Member's Home Care

Initials

_____ If my home cannot be used for any reason for home-assistance services provided by an outside agency or a family member, I direct my Health Care Representative to determine if a family member is able and willing to take care of me in his or her home.

_____ When a family member provides home-assistance services to me and I reside with that family member is his or her home, I direct, upon request in writing to my Health Care Representative by this family member, that my Health Care Representative submit a reasonable compensation request to the Trustee of my living trust as a health care expense.

_____   During any time when a family member provides home-assistance services and I reside with that family member in his or her home, I direct my Representative visit the home at least weekly to determine that the level of care I am receiving is appropriate.

Nursing Home/Institutional Care

Initials

_____   I do not wish to burden my family members with my health care needs. When I can no longer maintain my independent lifestyle, with occasional care from family members or home-assistance agencies, I wish to move to a nursing care facility, which can provide me with the appropriate level of care.

_____   During any time when my Health Care Representative believes that I can no longer receive appropriate care in my home or in a family member's home, I direct my Health Care Representative seek supporting certifications in writing from my primary care physician and an appropriate specialist recommended by my primary care physician and approved by my Health Care Representative. Upon receipt of these certifications, I authorize my Health Care Representative to select for me, and admit me into, a nursing care facility.

If I'm Disabled

Choosing a Nursing Care Facility

Initials

_____   If I must reside at a nursing care facility, to the extent it is economically feasible and medically advantageous, I direct my Health Care Representative to select the following facility:

_____

_____

Letter of Instruction to My Health Care Representative

_____ If that facility is not available or advisable in my Health Care Representative's sole discretion, my Health Care Representative should select a similar institution with the following qualities:

_____

_____

_____ When selecting a nursing care facility, I direct my Health Care Representative consider facilities that can provide me with the appropriate level of care while maintaining the greatest degree of independence that my condition may allow.

_____ When selecting a nursing care facility, I direct my Health Care Representative to first consider facilities located in the community where I live.

_____ When selecting a nursing care facility, I direct my Health Care Representative to first consider facilities located in the community where a majority of my family lives.

_____ When selecting a nursing care facility, I request that my Health Care Representative consult my family members to select a facility where my family members would feel comfortable visiting me.

_____ I would prefer, if possible, a nursing care facility that is operated in accordance with my religious beliefs.

_____ I qualify for admission to particular nursing care facilities because of my service as (veteran/clergy/other).

_____ I direct my Health Care Representative consult the following benefit program(s) when selecting a nursing care facility:

_____

_____

_____ I direct that my Health Care Representative make at least two unannounced visits to any prospective nursing care facilities to determine if the services are acceptable.

_____ My Health Care Representative shall inspect the credentials and abilities of care givers, the variety and nutritional value of meals, the type and frequency of recreational activities, the cleanliness of the facility, the frequency of visitors to the facility, and any other services my Representative shall determine important to the selection of a quality nursing care facility.

_____ During any time when I live in a nursing care facility, I direct that my Representative visit me to determine that the level of care I am receiving is appropriate.

_____ During any period of time that I might still be able to interact with facility residents and participate in activities, I direct that my Health Care Representative consider the following nursing care facility or other similar facility:

If I'm Disabled

_____

_____

_____

_____ During any period of time that I might be unable to interact with facility residents and participate in activities, I direct that my Health Care Representative consider the following nursing care facility or other similar facility:

_____

_____

_____

Medications

Initials

_____   I authorize my Health Care Representative to consent to medication to relieve my pain, if my primary care physician and specialists agree that the pain medication would not complicate or worsen my condition.

_____   I desire that my Health Care Representative be very cautious when consenting to any addictive medications.

_____   I prefer the use of natural vitamin and nutrition treatment whenever potentially beneficial to my condition.

_____   I do not wish to participate in any unconventional or experimental medication or therapy.

OR

_____   I authorize the use of unconventional or experimental medication or therapy, whenever possible.

- ❏ However, I am concerned about the high cost often associated with unconventional or experimental medication or therapy. I direct my Health Care Representative to balance the cost of the medication or therapy with the expected relief.
- ❏ I direct my Health Care Representative to consider any possible side effects associated with unconventional or experimental medication or therapy. I specifically do not want a "cure" that is worse than the original illness.

Medical Tests

Initials

_____   I direct my Health Care Representative not to allow any tests to be performed, if after consultation with my attending physician and any appropriate specialists, the suggested test results are not reasonably certain to be beneficial in restoring my health.

_____ I encourage my Health Care Representative to get second opinions from appropriate specialists, if economically feasible, before authorizing or not authorizing any testing that my attending physician or primary care physician believe would be beneficial in restoring my health.

Termination of Life Support Treatment

Initials

_____ In conjunction with the directions in my Living Will and Durable Medical Power of Attorney, I direct my Health Care Representative not to allow any medical procedure that, in the opinion of my attending physician, is considered heroic or beyond those procedures usually performed for people in my condition.

_____ When my Health Care Representative has consulted with my attending physician, and any other physicians necessary, and the conclusion is that medical treatment is only artificially prolonging the dying process or that there is no reasonable chance of regaining consciousness, I direct my Health Care Representative to authorize my attending physician to enter a "no-code" or "do not resuscitate" order on my medical records. My Health Care Representative should never feel guilty about authorizing this course of action because this is the decision I would make if I were able to do so myself.

_____ I direct my Health Care Representative to hold a conference with all willing and interested members of my immediate family prior to making any decision regarding termination of artificial life support treatments.

_____ I urge my Health Care Representative to consult the following individuals regarding termination of artificial life support treatments.

❏ Religious clergy _____
❏ Trusted friend _____
❏ Other _____

Letter of Instruction to My Health Care Representative

_____ I direct that my Health Care Representative consider the following concerns prior to making any decisions regarding termination of artificial life support treatments:

_____

_____

_____

_____

I have consulted with legal counsel, am fully informed as to all the contents of this document, and understand the full import of the grant of these instructions to the person or persons named in my Durable Medical Power of Attorney.

IN WITNESS WHEREOF, I have signed this Letter of Instruction to My Health Care Representative on: _____ / _____ / _____

Printed Name: _____

Signature: _____

Medical Intervention Definitions

Pain Medication: narcotics and drugs administered to reduce pain.

Antibiotic Treatment: the use of drugs to fight bacterial infection.

Blood Transfusion: the introduction of blood or blood plasma into a vein or artery.

Simple Diagnostic Test: blood test, X-rays, etc.

Invasive Diagnostic Test: a more complex test that may require cutting of the skin or the insertion of an instrument (cardiac catherization, etc.).

Chemotherapy: treatment of cancer with drugs, which may have substantial side effects.

Kidney Dialysis: medical removal of waste from blood.

Minor Surgery: a minor operative procedure.

Major Surgery: a more difficult and potentially dangerous procedure.

Organ Transplantation: replacement of a diseased organ with the organ of another person.

Mechanically-Assisted Breathing: may require the insertion of a tube into the windpipe.

Cardiopulmonary Resuscitation (CPR): techniques for stimulating a stopped heart.

Artificial Nutrition and Hydration: intravenous feeding, nasogastric intubation (feeding through a nose tube to the stomach), gastrostomy (feeding through a tube surgically implanted in the stomach).

Hypothetical Scenario Analysis

Record your preference by placing your initials in the box that best corresponds with your wishes. To eliminate any ambiguity regarding this scenario, please make certain you record a preferred course of action for each medical treatment or procedure.

Situation A

If I am in a coma or a persistent vegetative state and, in the opinion of my physician and several consultants, have no known hope of regaining awareness and higher mental functions no matter what is done, then my wishes regarding use of the following, if considered medically reasonable, would be:

Medical Treatment / Procedure	I want treatment	I want treatment, if no clear improvement, stop treatment	I am undecided	I do not want treatment
Cardiopulmonary Resuscitation				
Mechanical Breathing				
Artificial Nutrition and Hydration				
Major Surgery				
Minor Surgery				
Kidney Dialysis				
Chemotherapy				
Invasive Diagnostic Tests				
Blood or Blood Products				
Antibiotics				
Simple Diagnostic Tests				
Pain Medications *(Even if consciousness is dulled and indirectly shortens my life)*				

Notes _____

Situation B

If I am in a coma and, in the opinion of my physician and several consultants, I have a small likelihood of recovering fully, a slightly larger likelihood of surviving with permanent brain damage, and a much larger likelihood of dying, then my wishes regarding use of the following, if considered medically reasonable, would be:

Medical Treatment / Procedure	I want treatment	I want treatment, if no clear improvement, stop treatment	I am undecided	I do not want treatment
Cardiopulmonary Resuscitation				
Mechanical Breathing				
Artificial Nutrition and Hydration				
Major Surgery				
Minor Surgery				
Kidney Dialysis				
Chemotherapy				
Invasive Diagnostic Tests				
Blood or Blood Products				
Antibiotics				
Simple Diagnostic Tests				
Pain Medications *(Even if consciousness is dulled and indirectly shortens my life)*				

Notes _____

_____

_____

_____

Hypothetical Scenario Analysis

Situation C

If I have brain damage or some brain disease that in the opinion of my physician and several consultants cannot be reversed and that makes me unable to recognize people or to speak understandably, and I also have a terminal illness, such as incurable cancer, that will likely be the cause of my death, then my wishes regarding use of the following, if considered medically reasonable would be:

Medical Treatment / Procedure	I want treatment	I want treatment, if no clear improvement, stop treatment	I am undecided	I do not want treatment
Cardiopulmonary Resuscitation				
Mechanical Breathing				
Artificial Nutrition and Hydration				
Major Surgery				
Minor Surgery				
Kidney Dialysis				
Chemotherapy				
Invasive Diagnostic Tests				
Blood or Blood Products				
Antibiotics				
Simple Diagnostic Tests				
Pain Medications *(Even if consciousness is dulled and indirectly shortens my life)*				

Notes _____

_____

_____

_____

Situation D

If I have brain damage or some brain disease that in the opinion of my physician and several consultants cannot be reversed and that makes me unable to recognize people or to speak understandably, but I have no terminal illness and I can live in this condition for a long time, then my wishes regarding use of the following, if considered medically reasonable, would be:

Medical Treatment / Procedure	I want treatment	I want treatment, if no clear improvement, stop treatment	I am undecided	I do not want treatment
Cardiopulmonary Resuscitation		Not Applicable		
Mechanical Breathing				
Artificial Nutrition and Hydration				
Major Surgery		Not Applicable		
Minor Surgery		Not Applicable		
Kidney Dialysis				
Chemotherapy				
Invasive Diagnostic Tests		Not Applicable		
Blood or Blood Products				
Antibiotics				
Simple Diagnostic Tests		Not Applicable		
Pain Medications *(Even if consciousness is dulled and indirectly shortens my life)*				

If I'm Disabled

Notes _____

_____

_____

Hypothetical Scenario Analysis

Do Not Resuscitate Notice

DO NOT RESUSCITATE ORDER IN EFFECT

DO NOT DIAL 911 EMERGENCY

DO NOT START CPR

DO NOT take any emergency action except to make me comfortable or to administer pain relief.

DO NOT send me to the hospital unless approved by my Health Care Representative or the physician named below.

IN CASE OF EMERGENCY CONTACT:

1. _____   Phone (_____)_____
2. _____   Phone (_____)_____
3. _____   Phone (_____)_____

Signature: _____   Date: _____

Disability Checklist For Me

If you see the signs that you may need help, why not enlist your helpers now so that they will be better prepared when you can no longer work with them?

❑ If I know I am going to need help in the future, have I sought out my helpers?

- Do my helpers know my advisor team?
- Do my helpers know where my important papers are?
- Do my helpers understand my needs and goals?
- Are my helpers willing to help?
- Are my helpers qualified to help?
- Do my helpers know where to turn for more help?
- Do my helpers need encouragement, apologies or forgiveness now for what lies ahead?

❑ If I know I am getting not so well, have I reviewed my plan to make sure it does what I want and need?

Maybe your helpers aren't as qualified or willing as you previously thought. Perhaps you want to change the provisions you've made for your care.

If you start to involve your helpers now, you will have the opportunity to make changes to your plan so that it will best meet your needs and goals.

- Do I need to change my helpers?
- Do I need to change my medical care instructions?
- Do I need to change provisions or distributions to my beneficiaries?
- Am I providing for my spouse? Children? Grandchildren? Charities? Pets?
- Am I providing for my ex-spouse or their children, either by design or by default?
- Does my plan exclude anyone, by design or by default?

Disability Checklist For Me

Disability Checklist For Helpers

❑ Locate Original Documents

Properly designed and drafted trusts and powers of attorney will include instructions on how to determine and document incapacity as well as instructions for providing for the incapacitated person and other family members. A well-rounded plan will also include instructions for "What if..."

- How do I determine my Principal's incapacity?
- How do I provide for my Principal?
- How do I provide for my Principal's family members?
- Who are my Principal's other helpers?
- Who are my Principal's trusted medical, financial and personal advisors?

❑ Execute Necessary Documents

Authority to act is not automatic. Banks, investment institutions, courts, government agencies and private care providers all have requirements that must be met to ensure that you are acting with the proper authority under the proper circumstances.

- Get legal guidance on the dos and don'ts of your appointment and authority.
- Get certification of my Principal's disability in accordance with the plan and applicable laws.
- Get certification of my authority to act.
- Accept jurisdiction of the court if I am serving as guardian or conservator.
- File and record documents if required to do so.
- Execute documents undoing everything should my Principal recover.

❑ Provide for Your Principal

Your Principal's written documents are your guide. If you cannot or will not follow them – not only to the letter but also in

the spirit and intention of the entire document – DO NOT ACCEPT THE APPOINTMENT. If you cannot continue to serve once you have accepted the appointment, renounce the appointment. Legal documents have legal consequences.

- Follow the instructions given, regardless of how I feel.
- Know whether I must provide my Principal with home care, hospice care or hospital care.
- Enforce or withhold medical procedures and medication when necessary.
- Enforce DO NOT RESUSCITATE (DNR) orders.
- Enforce advanced healthcare directives (Living Will) when necessary.
- Ensure that my Principal has proper safety, security, medical and personal care.
- Put long-term healthcare plans into action.
- Ensure that my Principal's spiritual and religious needs are met.

❏ Provide for Dependants and Family Members

Properly drafted trusts and powers of attorney will include instructions on how to care for family members when a person is incapacitated. These documents have legal consequences.

- Place minor dependants with guardians.
- Place other incapacitated family members with guardians or institutions.
- Provide for the health, education, maintenance and support of family members.
- Be aware of health concerns of my Principal's family.
- Provide for clergy or other counseling for family.

❏ Provide Financially for Your Principal and His/Her Family

Develop and revise your Principal's financial plan based on the continuing prognosis of your Principal using your Principal's advisor team. Planning mistakes at this stage may have long-term adverse consequences and may affect qualifications for entitlement programs. One of your fiduciary duties is to protect the best interests of your Principal. Part of that duty includes ensuring assets are properly utilized and protected.

- Use my Principal's advisor team to develop and revise the financial plan.
- Apply for third-party insurance benefits.
- Apply with local, state and federal entitlement programs such as Social Security and Medicaid, Veterans Administration, etc.
- Apply for assistance from organizations that specialize in my Principal's incapacity.
- Pursue compensation and restitution from responsible parties if applicable.
- Do not disrupt productive investments.
- Do not disrupt assets that are excluded for qualification for entitlement programs.
- Maintain accurate and detailed records of transactions.
- Do not commingle my Principal's assets with my assets at any time.
- Pay bills that need to be paid to protect assets.
- Postpone payment of bills when it is appropriate.

❑ Help for Me and the Other Helpers

Being a fiduciary for an incapacitated person can be very demanding and stressful even when duties are spread out among several helpers. To compound matters, not only do you have additional demands on your time, you are likely to be feeling and dealing with a certain amount of grief. Don't feel like you have to do it all yourself.

- Enlist the help of others.
- Monitor my mental health and that of the other helpers.
- Use my Principal's team of advisors.
- Do not cause my family to suffer unduly.
- Ask for help and information from people and institutions that specialize in my Principal's incapacity or condition.
- In the end, even though it is painful for me, I will be blessed for being a part of my Principal's life, honored to be chosen to help, and at peace for giving him/her what he/she wanted.

After I'm Gone

Getting My Ducks In A Row

First Steps When Someone Dies

Immediate Action – The First Five Days

- ❑ Contact a relative or friend who can spend the next few days with you if you are alone.
- ❑ Notify relatives and close friends.
- ❑ Review organ donation and other anatomical gift instructions and comply with wishes.
- ❑ Find and review memorial instructions and known funeral and burial / cremation wishes and make those arrangements. Also check for prepaid funeral plans.
- ❑ Arrange for care of dependents – guardians, babysitters, helpers.
- ❑ Arrange for pet care.
- ❑ Locate important papers.
- ❑ Read the Will and Letters of Instruction.
- ❑ Notify clergy.
- ❑ Inform family members of your new role.
- ❑ Contact decedent's employer to check on expected death benefits (life insurance, pension, 401(k), accidental death insurance, etc.). Obtain policy numbers.
- ❑ Contact business associates regarding continued operation of business if applicable.
- ❑ Notify landlord, if any.
- ❑ File mail forwarding notice with post office.
- ❑ Stop newspaper and magazine delivery.
- ❑ Arrange for lawn care and other home maintenance items.

Memorandum for Distribution of Tangible Personal Property

- ❑ Review automobile insurance for coverage.
- ❑ Make an appointment to meet with decedent's attorney.
- ❑ Notify newspaper – Obituary.
- ❑ Locate military papers (VA provides certain benefits, including an American flag).
- ❑ Keep good records of all expenses for funeral and last illness.

Shortly after death – The first two weeks

- ❑ Locate and review estate planning documents.
- ❑ Prepare and sign Successor Trustee Affidavit.
- ❑ File original Will with county probate clerk.
- ❑ Remove valuables from the residence and place of business and store safely.
- ❑ Consider changing locks on real estate if not occupied by the spouse or a primary beneficiary.
- ❑ Determine immediate cash needs for beneficiaries. Identify accounts where cash is immediately available.
- ❑ Check safe deposit box for important papers. Inventory the property in the box in the presence of a bank officer, then remove the contents and close the box.
- ❑ Obtain extra copy of affidavit for management purposes.
- ❑ Obtain Federal Tax ID number for the estate and administrative trust.
- ❑ Open checking account in name of estate or trust with new ID number.
- ❑ Contact bank for check writing authority on open accounts.
- ❑ Notify insurance companies / agents. Check credit cards and clubs in which deceased was a member for additional insurance.

- ❑ Notify company personnel department.
- ❑ Notify Social Security Administration and VA (if applicable).
- ❑ Hold Social Security checks received after date of death.
- ❑ Notify all advisors (legal, financial and tax).
- ❑ Order death certificates.
- ❑ Collect and cancel credit cards, newspapers, magazine subscriptions, etc. Ask for refunds if applicable.

Within 30 Days

- ❑ Identify, notify and/or make claims to appropriate parties that may pay a burial and/or a death benefit.
  - Social Security
  - Pension funds
  - VA benefits
  - Life insurance payable to the trust

- ❑ Begin your lists.
  - Locate all assets and prepare inventory
  - Review of titling of assets
  - Liabilities and due dates

- ❑ Check to make sure insurance liability coverage on residence, automobiles, personal property in storage, etc. is adequate.
- ❑ Review business agreements and business operations.

Within 60 Days

- ❑ Provide written notice to heirs and beneficiaries.
- ❑ Meet with advisors regarding distribution of property and tax returns.
- ❑ Obtain tax identification number for new trusts.

Within 9 Months
- ❏ Review the Memorandum for Distribution of Personal Property.
- ❏ Review the allocation and distribution of remaining assets.
- ❏ Determine if disclaimers are to be prepared and filed.
    - Do not apply for or accept any assets to be disclaimed.
- ❏ File Federal Estate Tax Form 706 and Colorado Estate Tax Return.
    - Distribute assets either into trusts or to beneficiaries.

Within 12 Months
- ❏ Review your estate plan with your attorney.

Critical Dates – Review
- ❏ File the Will within 10 days of date of death.
- ❏ File final income tax return for decedent by April 15 of the year following year of death.
- ❏ File the federal estate tax return within nine months from the date of death.

Notes _____
_____
_____
_____
_____

Memorandum for Distribution of Tangible Personal Property

Most states allow your personal effects to be distributed according to specific written instructions you have prepared in a Memorandum for Disposition of Tangible Personal Property.

This document allows you to leave specific personal effects to specified loved ones without having to go through the time and expense of amending your Trust or changing your Will. You should use it for things like a special piece of jewelry, an automobile, your fur coat, military medals, trophies, the TV/DVD combo, your old 33-1/3 record collection, the family pet, or the black velvet Elvis Presley painting.

There is no magic form to use as a Memorandum. A sample form is provided for your convenience but any piece of paper that is dated and signed by you is sufficient. You may change your Memorandum at any time. However, it is important that you carefully follow the instructions provided to assist you in completing it. Completed properly, your Trustee, Personal Representative, and loved ones should have little difficulty following your instructions.

The property description and the names, addresses, and relationship of the beneficiaries may be either in your handwriting or typed, but it is imperative that you SIGN AND DATE the Memorandum. You may make copies of the Memorandum for your convenience and that of your recipients. You should also send a copy to your attorney.

Anything that you don't want to put on the Memorandum will be distributed according the terms of your Trust or Will. Your family and loved ones will appreciate you detailing who gets what so they don't have to worry or fight about it after you're gone.

Take a few minutes right now. Think of who would really like a couple of items that you have and jot the information down on your Memorandum. If you're married, make sure you identify whether the person is to receive the item only if you are the second spouse to die or even if your spouse survives you.

I hereby make this memorandum for the purpose of disposing of certain items of my tangible personal property at my death.

If the recipient of a particular item of personal property does not survive me, such item shall be disposed of as though it had not been listed in this memorandum.

Description of Tangible Personal Property	Person to Receive Property, Address and Relationship
_____	_____
_____	_____
_____	_____
_____	_____
_____	_____
_____	_____
_____	_____
_____	_____
_____	_____
_____	_____
_____	_____
_____	_____
_____	_____
_____	_____
_____	_____

Signature: _____ Date: _____

Letter of Instruction to My Guardian and Trustee

In order to assist the Guardian of my minor children and the Trustee of any Trust share created for my children under my estate planning documents, I leave these specific instructions to be incorporated by reference into the terms and conditions of the Trust.

Notification

Initials

_____   Upon my death, my Personal Representative shall deliver a copy of this Letter of Instruction to my Guardian and Trustee to:

- ❏ My children
- ❏ My children's Guardian
- ❏ My children's paternal/maternal grandparents
- ❏ Other: _____

Education

Initials

_____   *Preferred Type of Secondary Schooling:* If economically feasible, I prefer my children attend the following:

- ❏ public schools
- ❏ private schools
- ❏ private schools of my religious beliefs
- ❏ Other: _____

_____ *Academic Gifting Plan*: Each time my children receive a report card from the first grade of elementary education through the last year of high school, my Trustee shall distribute the following amounts to that child:

$ _____ for every "A" received,

$ _____ for every "B" received,

$ _____ for every "C" received.

_____ *Extracurricular Activities*: It is important to me that my children are able to participate in extracurricular activities. It is my desire that my Trustee provide economic assistance to enable my children to participate in extracurricular activities such as band, orchestra, sports, field trips, clubs, etc.

I specifically want my Trustee and my Guardian to encourage my children to participate in the following activities:

_____

_____

_____ *Specialized Academic Programs*: I authorize and encourage my Trustee to pay for any accelerated or remedial programs my children may qualify for or need.

Notes _____
_____
_____
_____
_____
_____

College

Initials

_____   *Savings Requirement*: During any period when my Trustee makes a distribution of net income or principal for the education needs of my children, any distribution shall be limited to an amount equal to the following:

❑ an amount equal to the amount the child has saved for education.

❑ An amount equal to twice the amount the child has saved for education.

❑ Other: _____

❑ My Trustee shall inspect account statements or other financial records to determine the amount the child has saved for education.

_____   *In-State Tuition Equivalent*: Any distribution for education shall be an amount equal to the then average costs of tuition, room, board, lab fees and required course materials at a state-supported college or university, as determined by my Trustee in its sole and absolute discretion. If my child elects to attend a private college or university, my Trustee shall distribute to such child only that amount equivalent to the average costs at a state-supported college or university, and the child may secure alternate means for financing any excess costs.

_____   *Qualifying Grade Requirement*: If my children receive a "D" or an "F" (or an equivalent grade on an alternative grading system) in a college, university, or vocational course, my Trustee shall subtract an amount equal to the cost of the credit hours for this course from the amount that child is eligible to receive for education needs in the next semester.

❑ My trustee may, in its sole and absolute discretion, make exceptions to this condition

Letter of Instruction to My Guardian and Trustee

when my child has been injured, ill, or suffered other disruptive circumstances.

_____   *Study-Abroad Programs*: If financially feasible, all or any part of my children's college education may be taken in a university located in a foreign country.

I would especially like to encourage a university in the following countries:

_____

_____

_____   *Four-year Incentive*: I direct my Trustee to make a special distribution of $ _____ to each of my children upon their completion of an undergraduate degree from an accredited college or university if completed within four (4) years or less.

Visitation

Initials

_____   *Family*: To the extent that distance will allow, it is very important to me that my children shall have equal contact with both maternal and paternal sides of the family. The term "family" includes children's grandparents, aunts, uncles and cousins.

- ❏ It is important to communicate with grandparents via telephone or letter at least (circle one):
  weekly / monthly / annually / other: _____

- ❏ It is important to physically get together with grandparents at least (circle one):
  weekly / monthly / annually / other: _____

- ❏ It is important to communicate with family at least (circle one):
  weekly / monthly / annually / other: _____

❏ It is important to physically get together with family at least (circle one):
weekly / monthly / annually / other: _____

_____ *Supervision*: Under no circumstances, shall the Guardian allow any of my children to visit with _____ unless the Guardian is also present during the entire visit.

_____ *Travel*: Before my minor children are able to travel alone, the Trustee is directed to pay for either the Guardian or another family member to meet the traveling child and accompany the child to the travel destination.

_____ *Holidays*: Holidays are important to our family and for that reason, my children are to spend some time with our families on holidays (Christmas, Easter, Thanksgiving and birthdays). It is my desire that an acceptable arrangement be worked out between all families concerned.

❏ However, if not, the children will alternate the holidays between both families starting with either the maternal side or the paternal side on Thanksgiving and Christmas in even years, and then with the other side on Thanksgiving and Christmas in odd years.

Other: _____

_____

_____

_____

_____

_____

_____

_____

Guardian

Initials

_____ *Payment*: As compensation, on each anniversary of the date my children began living with their Guardian, my Trustee, upon the written request of such Guardian, shall pay to such Guardian as compensation for caring for my children an amount not to exceed $_____.

- ❏ This annual compensation shall continue until my youngest child reaches the age of _____ or completes high school, whichever occurs first.

- ❏ Such compensation shall be paid from the net income of the trust and under no circumstances shall my Trustee invade the trust principal to pay such Guardian's compensation. In the event the trust net income for any year shall not equal the amount of compensation requested by the Guardian, the Guardian's compensation for that year shall be the amount of trust net income earned in that anniversary year.

_____ *Vacation*: As compensation for caring for my children, my Trustee may make an annual distribution for any expenses incurred by the Guardian for a vacation enjoyed by both the Guardian's family and my children.

_____ *Children's Biological Parent as Guardian*: When, if ever, my children are in the physical custody of their biological parent, my Trustee shall be very conservative when distributing for the children's health, education, maintenance and support needs. My Trustee shall determine other resources available to my children through the support of their biological parent. It is my desire that the preservation of principal be a priority and that genuine need must be shown by my children before my Trustee shall make a discretionary distribution. My purpose for requiring this limited access during any period of time that my children live in the custody of their biological parent is based on my desire to prevent the use of any trust assets from supplanting my ex-spouse's financial responsibility of supporting my children's needs during their years as a minor dependent.

Religion

Initials

_____ I prefer my children be raised in this faith: _____

_____ However, this preference is intended to be flexible to accommodate the regular church involvement of the children's Guardian, and it is my overriding intention that my children and the Guardian attend church as a family.

Safety Concerns

Initials

_____ *Automobiles*: If the Guardian or my Trustee decide to give any of my children an automobile, such automobile must be considered "reliable and safe" according to automobile analyst sources, such as *Consumer Reports* magazine or other such publication.

_____ *Firearms*:

❑ My children are not to be permitted to own or use firearms of any kind.

❑ Prior to handling firearms, my child is to receive professional instruction on firearm safety.

Counseling

Initials

_____ *Grief Counseling*:

❑ Due to the impressionable age of my children, I caution my Trustee and Guardian to be vigilant in observing signs of distress or difficulty in coping with the situation after my death.

❑ I specifically authorize my Trustee to provide for grief and/or suicide counseling for any or all of my children if my Trustee and Guardian determine such counseling to be in the best interest of my children.

_____ *Self-Esteem Counseling*: While in early adolescence, my children are to take assertiveness training classes in order to build strong self-esteem.

_____ *Budgeting Restrictions*: I believe that budgeting is an important step to responsible financial management.

❑ When my children reach age _____, they are to each take budgeting lessons or courses.

❑ Prior to establishing a separate trust share for each of my children, my Trustee shall recommend a budget counselor for each child to consult and shall encourage each child to receive budget counseling.

❑ Despite any conflicting provisions in the Trust, I direct that prior to receiving any income or principal from the separate trust share created under the trust, each of my children shall consult with a budget counselor approved by my trustee.

❑ If my child creates and lives within the bounds of his or her budget for consecutive days, then my Trustee may distribute any income and principal to the child from his or her trust share in accordance with the terms and conditions of the trust.

❑ My Trustee may rely on the written statement of the budget counselor that after creation of the budget, my child lived within its bounds for _____ consecutive days.

- When selecting a budget counselor, I encourage my Trustee to consider an individual or member of an organization bonded and licensed under the Budget Service Companies Act.

- When selecting an acceptable budget counselor, I encourage my Trustee to consider the following:

  _____
  _____
  _____
  _____

- My Trustee, in its sole discretion, is authorized, but not directed, to pay any costs associated with the budget counseling process.

Financial Investment Instruction: It is my strong belief that financial education is critical to my children's ability to make optimal use of inherited funds. To this end, in all matters concerning the investment of funds distributed to my children, it is my desire that:

- When my children reach age _____, they each are to take financial planning courses.

- My children should consult regularly with a financial advisor regarding investment matters. The financial advisor selected shall possess qualifications that include, at a minimum, attainment of the Certified Financial Planner (CFP) designation.

- The financial advisor selected shall possess the following additional qualifications:

  _____
  _____
  _____

- ❏ Prior to establishing a separate trust share for each of my children, my Trustee shall recommend a basic financial planning course or seminar for each child to attend and shall encourage the child to attend.

- ❏ Despite any conflicting provision in the trust, I direct that prior to receiving any income or principal from the separate trust share created under the trust, each of my children shall consult with a financial planner approved by my Trustee.

- ❏ Once my child has established a financial plan through the planner approved by my Trustee, then my Trustee may distribute any income and principal to the child from his or her trust share in accordance with the terms of my trust.

Notes _____

_____

_____

_____

_____

_____

_____

_____

_____

Dated: _____

Printed Name: _____

Signature: _____

Social Security

Social Security benefits should be applied for as soon as possible following the death of a wage earner. You will need to take with you the following documents:

- ❑ Death Certificate
- ❑ Marriage License
- ❑ Previous divorce papers of deceased
- ❑ Birth Certificates of deceased, spouse, children (including step-children living in the household of the deceased)
- ❑ Military discharge papers
- ❑ Income Tax Returns – previous two years
- ❑ Social Security numbers of deceased, spouse, children (including step-children living in household of deceased)

Full Name	Social Security Number
_____	_____
_____	_____
_____	_____
_____	_____
_____	_____
_____	_____
_____	_____
_____	_____

Instructions for Final Arrangements

These pages focus on leaving instructions for your loved ones regarding the myriad of tasks and responsibilities that come about because of your death.

Properly completed, this worksheet will be an invaluable resource for your loved ones. It will help them make good decisions, with clearly defined parameters of your desires when the shock of your death is still fresh, the grief process has just begun and they likely are not thinking clearly. It will also help unify the decision–making process among your loved ones and will greatly reduce family arguments over these matters.

One of the goals of this section is to help ensure that 60 days after you're gone your family is still hugging one another instead of at odds and fighting with one another.

If you need additional room to put something that's not on the list, just cross out something you don't need and write in what you do need. Of course, if you need additional sheets go ahead and add them.

That's it. This checklist is simple to complete and yet so important for your loved ones. Make copies of your checklist for your convenience and that of your loved ones. You should also send one to your attorney.

Take a few minutes right now and complete the worksheet. It's important to you and to your loved ones that you give them some clue of your wishes, wants and desires BEFORE they need it so they don't have to wonder what to do and where to start after your death. Without this critical worksheet, it's anybody's guess what'll happen!

To My Loved Ones

I am writing this letter to simplify matters for you when I die. It expresses my wishes and beliefs regarding my memorial and funeral arrangements and such things so no one has to guess (or fight about) what my desires were.

It is my intent that my Trustee, Personal Representative, and loved ones follow the instructions contained in these pages. I recognize, however, that there are circumstances that I cannot anticipate. It is my hope that my Trustee, Personal Representative, and loved ones will use their best abilities to carry out these instructions.

I am of sound mind and lawful age. I hereby revoke all prior Declarations, Wills, Codicils, Trusts, Powers of Appointment, and Powers of Attorney insofar as they relate to the disposition of my last remains. I declare and direct that after my death the following provisions be taken:

1. *Conflicts with My Living Trust or Pour-Over Will*

    If any instruction contained in this letter is in conflict with any of provision of my Trust or Will, the provisions of my Trust or Will, as the case may be, shall control.

2. *Notification of My Death*

    - Upon my death, please notify the following relatives, friends and organizations:

    _____

    _____

    _____

    _____

    _____

    _____

- I would like to have my obituary placed in the following newspapers, newsletters, etc.

  _____

  _____

  _____

  _____

- Other notification instructions:

  _____

  _____

  _____

3. *Information for My Obituary*

    - My Date of Birth: _____
    - My Place of Birth: _____
    - My Family:

      Maternal Grandparents:

      _____   _____

      Paternal Grandparents:

      _____   _____

      Parents:

      _____   _____

      Siblings:

      _____

      _____

      _____

      _____

Spouse:

_____

      We were married on: _____

      We were married at: _____

Children:

_____

_____

_____

_____

_____

Grandchildren:

_____

_____

_____

_____

_____

_____

_____

_____

_____

_____

_____

- Schools attended, graduation dates, degrees, honors:

_____

_____

_____

_____

_____

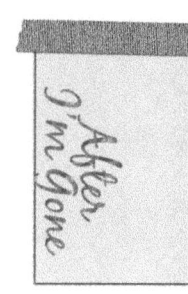

To My Loved Ones

- Social and civic organizations and offices held:

  _____
  _____
  _____
  _____

- Where I worked and positions held:

  _____
  _____
  _____
  _____
  _____
  _____
  _____

- Professional organizations and offices held:

  _____
  _____
  _____
  _____

- Religious affiliations and offices held:

  _____
  _____
  _____
  _____

- Churches attended:

  _____
  _____
  _____
  _____

- Other information for my obituary:

  _____
  _____
  _____
  _____
  _____
  _____
  _____
  _____
  _____
  _____
  _____
  _____
  _____
  _____
  _____
  _____
  _____

4. *Funeral Home/Crematory*

   ❏ I have already made pre-need arrangements with the following funeral home/crematory:

   Name: _____

   Address: _____

   Phone: (_____) _____

   The documents regarding my pre-need arrangements are located: _____

   _____

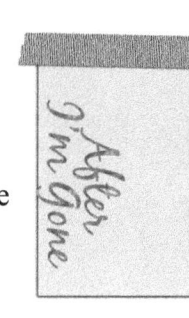

❑ I have not made any pre-need arrangements, but I would prefer you use the following funeral home/crematory:

Name: _____

Address: _____

Phone: (_____) _____

❑ Other funeral home/crematory instructions:

_____
_____
_____
_____
_____
_____

5. *Disposition of My Body*

I would like to be:
- ❑ Buried
- ❑ Cremated
- ❑ Entombed
- ❑ My body donated for scientific purposes
- ❑ Other disposition instructions: _____

_____
_____
_____
_____
_____

6. *Funeral/Memorial Service*

- ❏ I would like a funeral service if my body is present.
- ❏ Open casket
- ❏ Closed casket
- ❏ Viewing _____
- ❏ Wake _____
- ❏ I would like to have a Memorial Service instead of a funeral service if my body is not present.
- ❏ I DO NOT want any funeral or memorial service, but would request:
    - ❏ Direct cremation
    - ❏ Direct burial
- ❏ I would like the following in lieu of any of the above:

  _____
  _____
  _____

- ❏ I would like my funeral/memorial service to be held at the following facility:

  Name: _____
  Address: _____

- ❏ I would like the following person(s) to officiate at my funeral/memorial service:

  _____
  _____

❑ I would like the following person(s) to give my eulogy, homily or words of comfort at my memorial service:

_____

_____

_____

❑ I would like my funeral/memorial service to be:

    ❑ Open to the publication

    ❑ Open only to my family and close friends

    ❑ Open only to: _____

    _____

❑ I would like the have the following additional ceremony:

_____

_____

_____

    ❑ Held at the following location:

    _____

    _____

❑ I would like the following music/video selections played at my service:

_____

_____

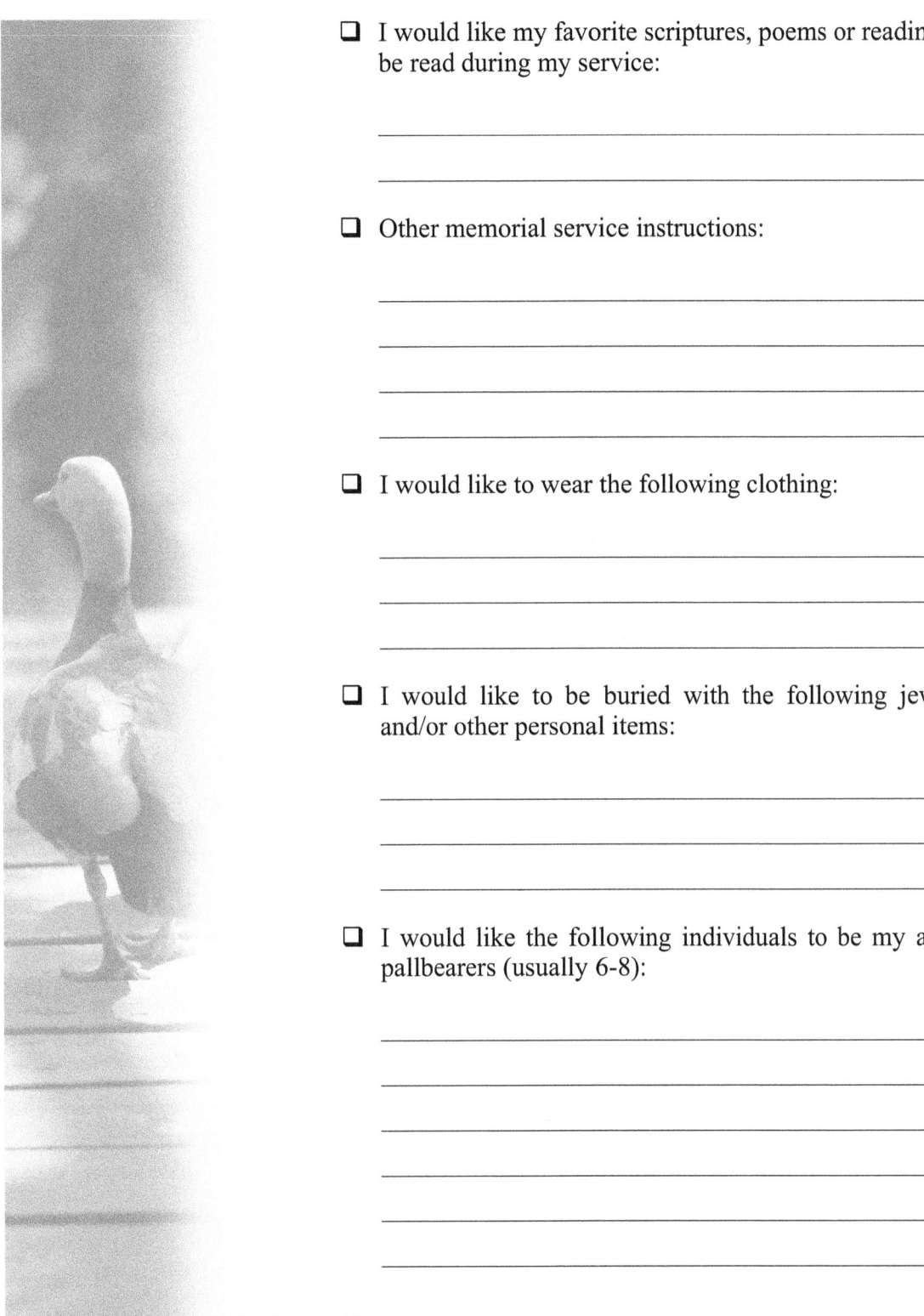

- ❑ I would like my favorite scriptures, poems or readings to be read during my service:

  _____

  _____

- ❑ Other memorial service instructions:

  _____

  _____

  _____

  _____

- ❑ I would like to wear the following clothing:

  _____

  _____

  _____

- ❑ I would like to be buried with the following jewelry and/or other personal items:

  _____

  _____

  _____

- ❑ I would like the following individuals to be my active pallbearers (usually 6-8):

  _____

  _____

  _____

  _____

  _____

❏ I would like the following honorary pallbearers:

_____
_____
_____
_____
_____
_____

❏ I would like the following people to be flower bearers:

_____
_____
_____
_____

❏ Other funeral/memorial service instructions:

_____
_____
_____
_____
_____
_____

7. *Burial/Entombment/Inurnment*

❏ I would like my final disposition to be made at the following cemetery/mausoleum:

Name: _____
Address: _____
Phone: (_____) _____

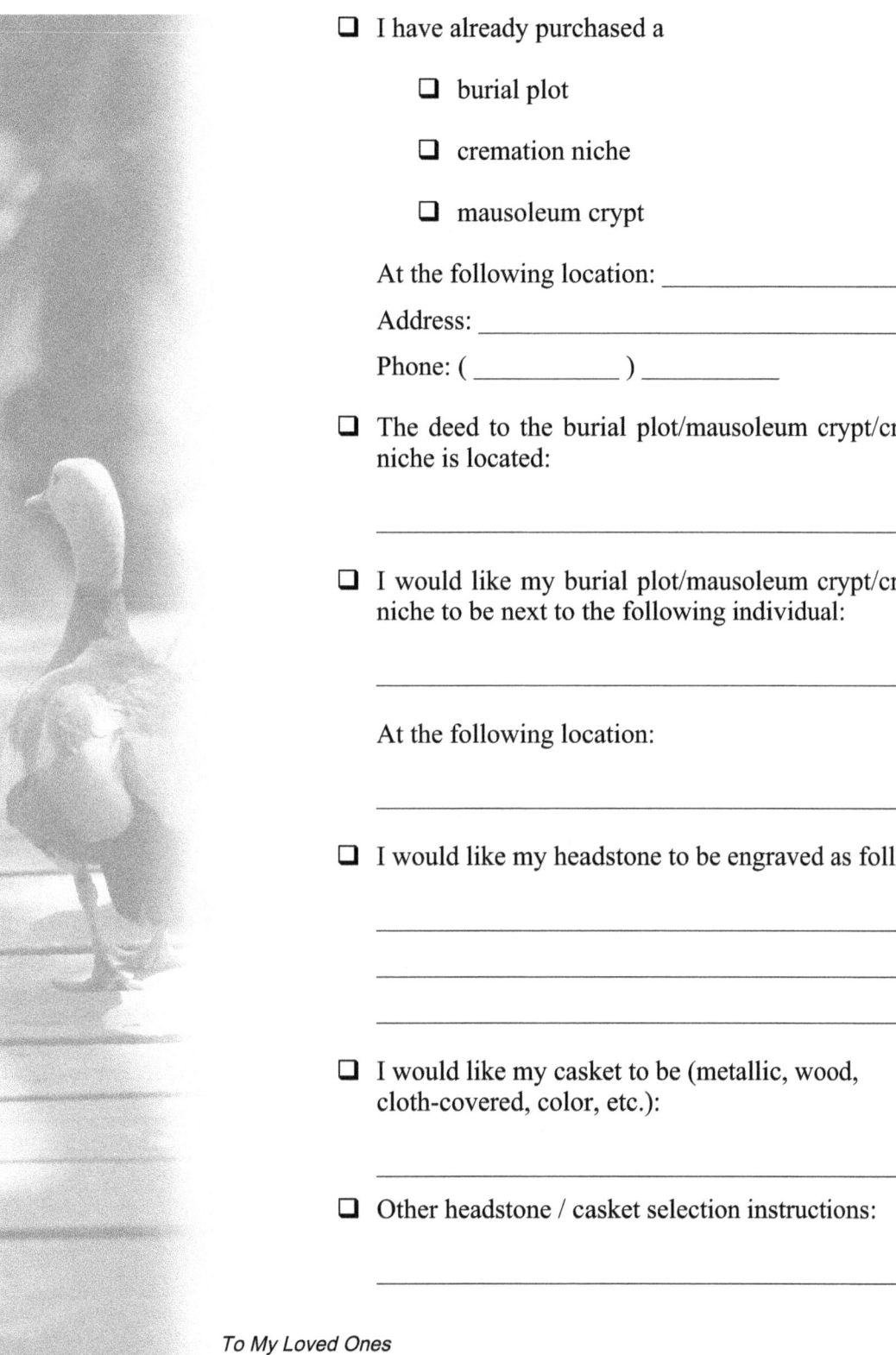

- ❑ I have already purchased a

    - ❑ burial plot
    - ❑ cremation niche
    - ❑ mausoleum crypt

    At the following location: _____

    Address: _____

    Phone: (_____) _____

- ❑ The deed to the burial plot/mausoleum crypt/cremation niche is located:

    _____

- ❑ I would like my burial plot/mausoleum crypt/cremation niche to be next to the following individual:

    _____

    At the following location:

    _____

- ❑ I would like my headstone to be engraved as follows:

    _____
    _____
    _____

- ❑ I would like my casket to be (metallic, wood, cloth-covered, color, etc.):

    _____

- ❑ Other headstone / casket selection instructions:

    _____

To My Loved Ones

8. *Final Expenses*

- ❏ I would like my final expenses to be:
    - ❏ economical
    - ❏ moderate
    - ❏ elaborate
- ❏ Other final expense instructions:

    _____
    _____
    _____
    _____

I have executed this declaration as my free and voluntary act on the date indicated below.

I may revoke or amend this declaration in writing at any time. I agree that a third party who receives a copy of this Declaration may act according to it. Revocation of the Declaration is not effective as to a third party until the third party learns of my revocation. My estate shall indemnify any third party for costs incurred as a result of claims that arise against the third party because of good-faith reliance on this declaration.

Thank you for doing your best to see that my wishes are carried out.

Dated: _____

Printed Name: _____

Signature: _____

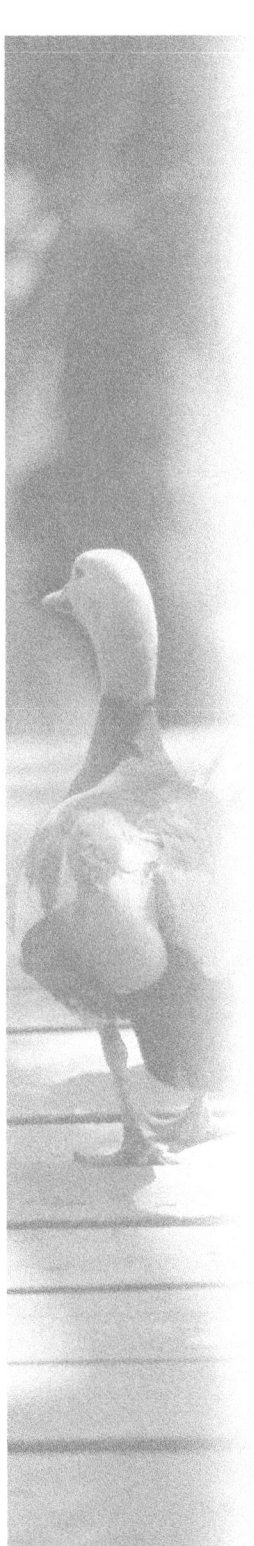

Notes:

Notes:

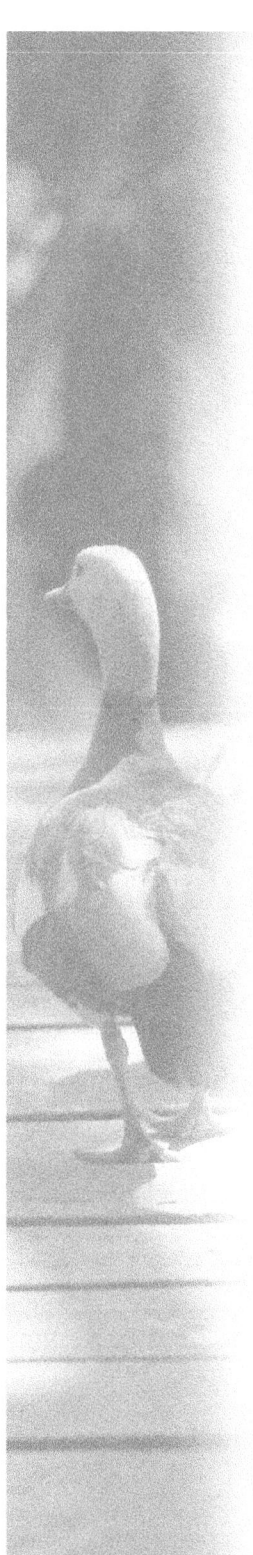

Notes:

Notes:

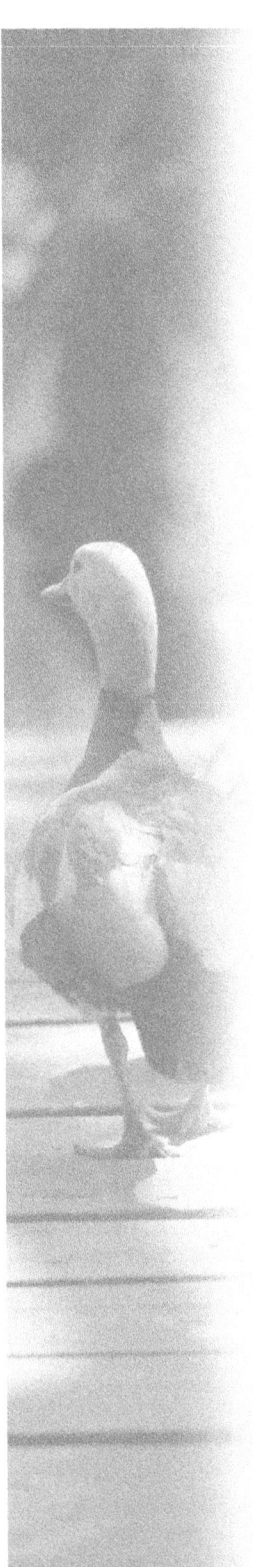

Notes:

Notes:

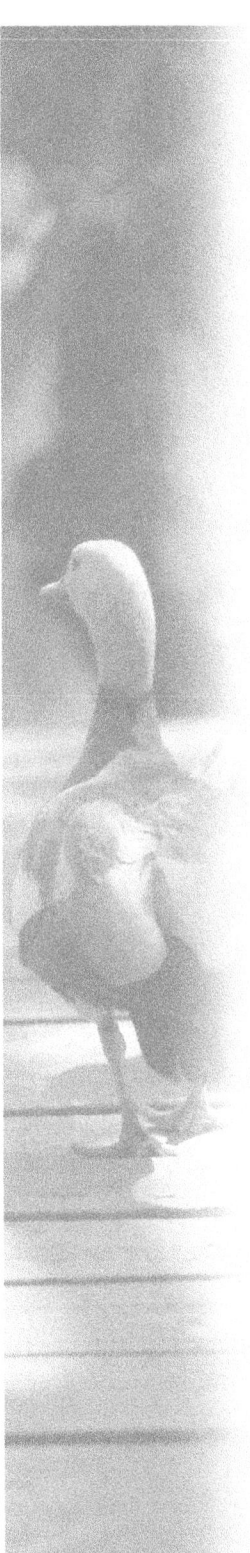

Notes:

Notes:

www.ingramcontent.com/pod-product-compliance
Lightning Source LLC
LaVergne TN
LVHW061215060426
835507LV00016B/1940